AFTER THE CRISIS:
HOW DID THIS HAPPEN?

*English translation by ESKA Publishing and Katrin Holt, Lily Heise,
Arnold Gremy and Paul and Jack Lipscomb.
A special thanks to Katrin Holt, Lily Heise, Arnold Gremy and
Paul and Jack Lipscomb for their editing support.
Published with the support of CNL – National Book Center – Paris.*

© **2010 ESKA PUBLISHING WASHINGTON – EDITIONS ESKA PARIS**
for the Publisher Consultant Paul Lipscomb
3808 SW Dosch Road, Portland, Oregon, 97239 - USA
paullips3@gmail.com

ISBN 978-2-7472-1548-0

Distribution World Wide:
ESKA Publishing
12, rue du Quatre-Septembre
75002 Paris - France
Tel: +33 (0)1 42 86 55 65
Fax: +33 (0)1 42 60 45 35
http://www.eska.fr

Distribution in North America:
IPM: International Publishers Marketing
22841 Quicksilver Drive, Dulles, VA 20166
USA
Tel: 703-661-1531
Fax: 703-661-1547
www.internationalpublishermarket.com

Printed in Canada by Transcontinental

Jacques Attali

AFTER THE CRISIS:
HOW DID THIS HAPPEN?

ESKA
Publishing

TABLE OF CONTENTS

Insufficient Demand, Debt-Created Demand, The Drop in Interest Rates, Leverage and Wealth Effect, Frantic Pursuit of Savings: Securitization and Derivative Products, Insurers Create CDSs and Monolines to Overcome the Difficulty of Attracting Capital, The Blindness of Credit Rating Agencies, The Explosion of Global Debt, Those who had Foreseen the Crisis, Why Didn't We Listen to Them?, Finance and Cocaine, The Reversal of the Subprime Market – The Economy of Panic, Chronology

The New Stakes of the Financial System, Threatened Insurers, Estimates, The Recession, Depression,

Bankruptcy of Developed Countries and the Future of "Chimerica", Exchange Crisis, The Social, Ideological and Political Crisis

Markets, Democracy and "Insiders", Disloyalty and the Rule of the Financier, The Disappearance of the Rule of Law, The Triumph of Financial Capitalism, The Triggering of a Financial Crisis, The Solution: Rebalancing the Market by a Rule of Law

Restore Order in Each National Economy, Strengthen European Regulation, Set up a Global Financial Regulation System, International Governance, Large-scale Worldwide Public Works

Financial Crises to Come, Other Dangers: the Future of Complex Global SystemsIntroduction

INTRODUCTION

How did this happen? Everything seemed to be going well in the world; political liberty and individual initiative seemed to be blossoming even in the most remote corners of the earth. In Asia and Latin America, poverty seemed to be decreasing and the world's economic growth was the fastest ever in history; everything led us to believe that this was going to continue for several decades, thanks to a strong demographic boom, abundant savings and outstanding technological progress which would also redirect it towards more sustainable development.

Then, without any warning, we find ourselves at the dawn of the most serious planetary recession for eighty years.

Between these two events, nothing seemed to happen except that some American families found themselves unable to continue to repay their mortgages.

The goal of this book is to explain this mystery as simply as possible, to anticipate where it is taking us, and to make sure that this does not happen again. In order to do that, we must put recent events into their historical context, solve the enigma that surrounds the reasons for panic, give a new point of view on the crisis, and on what the future has in store.

Since what cannot be expressed in a few words cannot be explained clearly, here is a summary of the content of this book in a few lines, then in a few pages.

Firstly in a few lines:

This first globalization crisis can be explained to a great extent by America's inability to pay its middle classes a decent salary, therefore inciting them to borrow money to buy their homes and increasing the value of property and production. Financial institutions and "insiders," who run the market, allocate themselves the majority of the ensuing wealth without any supervision from central banks, governments or international institutions, and so without running any risk, thanks to securitization (CDOs[1]) and a pseudo-insurance (a CDS). In return, this allows indebtedness to grow until it becomes intolerable and incites panic, loss of confidence and avoidance of all debt. From this a profound planetary depression could soon emerge, or on the contrary, a period of harmonious growth could begin. The latter would imply real debt reduction rather than the transfer of debt to taxpayers, as has already begun. It would

---

[1] See glossary: page 213.

mainly require that the power of the market be balanced by democracy, and that, on a planetary scale. That the power of the financial markets be balanced by law; that the power of "insiders" be balanced by that of citizens. There is still time for that: we can forestall an avalanche, we cannot stop it.

Now this can also be summed up in a few pages[2]:

Humanity has always undergone crisis situations, whether they be religious, moral, political or economic. Ever since capitalism came to power, the state of crisis could even be described as the norm. We can all feel, however, that a major shock is under way, that a widespread depression is looming, like a terrible surprise lurking in a world full of promise and we can all sense that our way of life and our social organization are being profoundly yet confusingly changed.

In my opinion, today's crisis can be explained simply: even though the market is the best way of sharing rare resources, it is incapable of its own accord of creating the necessary rule of law and the demand needed for the means of production to be used to their full capacity. In order for a market society to work effectively, there must be a rule of law that guarantees the law of ownership, that enforces sustainable competition, and that creates a demand through decent salaries and public orders; this would imply a political intervention, if possible

---

[2] Also in table form: see pages 219-224.

11

democratic rather than totalitarian, in the distribution of income and personal assets. The lack of ability to enforce this improved distribution of income has meant the emergence of a demand sustained by the indebtedness of ordinary employees, which was itself secured by property bought with that same debt. This has been happening for at least twenty years, particularly in America. In order to make this indebtedness bearable, the Central American Bank had to drop interest rates from 2001 onwards, therefore supplying a new source of wealth to those who knew how to invest borrowed money and make a profit from it. Private financial institutions, and the "insiders" who run them, wanted to insure themselves against the risks created by these new debts, as well as maximizing their profits. To do this, they put in place very complex insurance policies (such as CDSs and monolines) and even more complex securitization policies, (CDOs and ABSs) the importance of which I will explain later. This allows the risk to be transferred to other banks and financial institutions the world over, and to investors who do not understand them. Once again, there is no control. The United States of America ranks first place amongst these financial market and data control masters. America is increasingly living beyond its means, and this is financed by China (through blocked savings in the form of American treasury bonds, that cannot be sold without the risk of the dollar collapsing, which would destroy the competitiveness of the Chinese export industry), and Europe, (through blocked savings in European banks, in the form of securitizations and insurance).

From 1990 onwards, this high profitability and risk transfer were strongly encouraged by investment funds, (capital or speculative) which needed higher and higher profit margins in order to satisfy the unlimited greed of their investors. This was also encouraged by pension funds, which were becoming more demanding on account of the ageing of the population

At the same time, in California, everything was going well, American technological feats on the Internet were still fascinating the world, so nobody could see that essential talent and important capital were being diverted away from industry and research in favor of the financial system itself.

The financial arrangers of the products destined for the lenders and borrowers (the "insiders" as I call them) felt that this could not last forever, so they increased the amount they deducted from any profit generated.

At the other end of the social scale, the poorest and most indebted American households, who had been offered new mortgages, subprimes, a name chosen to show that these are 'second chance' loans, thought that they were overcoming poverty by accepting to borrow money secured by the increase in the value of their homes. At the same time, the institutions that had issued these loans were regrouping them as securities and passing the risk onto other savers. From winter 2006 onwards, lots of these people found that they could no longer reimburse their loans.

All securitized assets started to raise doubts from mid-2007 onwards, but rating agents had not noticed anything, nor had the IMF made any comment, nor had it been mentioned by the G8. American banks, then Swiss, then American again, then English, Belgian, German, and French banks, discovered, as if they had had no idea, what was on their balance sheets. Indeed, rather a lot of them. The American Federal agencies in charge of housing, then insurance companies and finally savers all started to panic. All wanted to rid themselves of debt. Many countries saw their capital flee; banks in developed countries were worried about what other toxic products they might find in their accounts and stopped granting loans to many healthy companies. Those banks and countries, which, up until then, had not hesitated in financing American deficits, started wondering about what they had been doing.

At the beginning of September 2008, the confident economy became an economy of panic. A major financial crisis exploded. This crisis was the opportunity to see that the system was corrupt, paying handsomely those who control and evaluate it, and allocating obscene salaries to those responsible for these disasters. Fear took hold more strongly. All tried to protect themselves by saving more and refusing to take any more risks. Interbank markets closed. Typically, this is the moment that the governments chose to announce that all was well. Not being under any illusion, the citizens could see that there was a catastrophe just around the corner. These thoughts precipitated it.

On October 3, 2008, the world financial system narrowly escaped collapse, through lack of liquidities. On October 13, the G8 governments announced that they were going to supply their banks with resources that they did not have. After a tremendous ideological pile-up, American and English banks and insurance companies were saved by nationalizations and a promise of nonexistent public funds. The private debt became a public debt.

However, nothing has been solved and the crisis is only just beginning, recession is here, debt reduction is speeding up and depression is looming. If nothing is done, it will profoundly affect businesses, consumers, workers, savers, borrowers, towns and nations. After having seen their shareholders' equity capital disappear, banks are worried about their future and are refusing to lend money to perfectly healthy businesses, which will therefore go bankrupt. The banks themselves will have to reduce their loans or be nationalized. China, following Japan's lead, has been helping America make ends meet, but it will slowly start to repatriate its savings. The United States will no longer be able to find anyone to finance their debt, the only solution will be to fall back on a moratorium or on inflation, but both options would ruin all those with any capital, and would make the dollar, already discredited by American foreign debt, collapse.

Depression is threatening for two, perhaps five or even ten years; the time it takes for the countries of the western world to rid themselves of their debt. This depression will bring with it a huge price crash that even a revival of public spending will not be able to slow down.

The world financial crisis, now an economic crisis, will change to a major social and political crisis and hundreds of millions of people will be threatened by unemployment. The very political regime will be criticized and rejected for being incapable of managing its "golem:" the market that it helped to create. Then inflation will arrive, violently. All the ideology of our individualist and disloyal societies will be reassessed, and democracy along with it.

If we want to avoid history taking this terrible route, it is time to understand that the source can be found in the imbalance between the market and the rule of law: this imbalance reduces demand, transfers it to debt and creates major financial annuities, whether they be legal, " a-legal," illegal or even criminal. The "insiders," who are perfectly aware of the risk that the world is running due to anarchical market development, are doing everything in their power to enhance their profits, like thieves hurrying to run off with as much gold as they can from the bank's safe, taking all risks in the last seconds of a hold-up before the police arrive. It is time to understand that today taxpayers are paying bonuses to the bankers who got them into such a situation. It is also time to realize that this crisis could be a stroke of luck for the world, a last alarm bell warning against the dangers of anarchical and wasteful globalization.

It is time to become aware that we have at our disposal the human, financial and technological means enabling us to limit this crisis so that it is only a slight setback, that we will only pull through if economic and financial information is equally shared out and available to everybody at the same time, if financial markets, global by nature, are balanced by a planetary rule of law, if this financial casino ceases, if a banker's job becomes modest and boring again, as it never should have stopped being, if a real risk assessment and liquidity requirements are put in place on a worldwide scale, if it is decided that the system of compensation will be revised and market and banking activities separated, if it decided that the people who cause others to run risks should be personally involved in the venture, and if we can set up, on a planetary scale, environment-friendly, large-scale public works, which up until now has only been done on the scale of some countries.

Unfortunately, it would seem that hardly anything of the kind will be done in time.

Yet, just as the "tulip crisis" paved the way for one hundred and fifty years of tremendous growth in the

Dutch Republic in 1637, the subprime crisis, the first real globalization crisis, could considerably hasten the realization that one day it will be necessary to set up a socialization of the most important monetary markets, which are the instruments of sovereignty, with an equal access to knowledge, a stable world market, a world minimum wage, and a world rule of law, as a prelude to an eventual world government.

We are separated from this obvious fact by at most a century, and, no doubt, numerous other crises and wars.

CHAPTER 1

LESSONS LEARNT FROM PAST CRISES

Humanity has always undergone crisis situations, whether they be religious, moral, political or economic. Ever since capitalism came to power, the state of crisis could even be described as the norm.

We can all feel, however, that a major shock is under way, that depression is looming, like a terrible surprise lurking in a world full of promise and we can all sense that our way of life and our social organization are being profoundly yet confusingly changed.

But, how did this come about? In this particular crisis, everyone has a preconceived opinion, be it political or ideological, that they want to impose. These opinions vary from the crisis being a sign that globalization is failing, whilst others believe that it is the proof of the necessity to expand globalization further than ever before. The crisis is reportedly an alarm bell telling us to put an end to bureaucracy or to enforce a collective, planetary regulation, or even appropriation. It reportedly forecasts inflation, or threatens deflation. It makes us realize how harmful debt can be, or quite the opposite, encourages us to borrow more, or it is said to prove the importance of competition between private banks, or to show the necessity to nationalize them.

The present financial crisis is not the first that history has known. It is just the first to take on a planetary dimension. It is also starting to become an economic crisis. It is not yet a monetary crisis. Like everything that has ever befallen humanity, for good or for evil, this crisis is larger, deeper, more brutal, and more powerful than any of its predecessors. In the brief history of our future, it will be a time of acceleration rather than a change of course.

In order to understand this crisis, we must look back to past events of the same type.

Since the beginning of capitalism in the 12th century in Bruges, each major financial crisis has begun in the financial capital of the moment, which generally, is also the economic and political "heart." The crisis begins by weakening the currency, the budget and the financial establishments of the "heart." This is followed by its consolidation, if the crisis has managed to bring in protective measures, or by the replacement of the "heart" if no other solution is found.

An example is the financial crisis of Genoa. Around 1620, this "heart" was the principal market for American silver and gold, but the market was weakened by the recession coming from Spain, of which Genoa was a satellite. Genoa could not prevent the Dutch and their new-found freedom from taking control of the Atlantic routes and enticing the American gold and silver to Amsterdam. For the third time, (after Bruges and Antwerp beforehand), the center of capitalism shifted towards the Atlantic. This was a point of no return. The Mediterranean was to become a secondary sea forever more and the countries surrounding it, including France, lost all physical contact with the "heart" forever. From that moment on, their standard of living would always be inferior to the new powers, and especially to Amsterdam, the new "heart."

Financial euphoria immediately hit Amsterdam and its as yet unregulated markets. In 1636, the tulip bulb, a symbol of wealth and luxury, became a source of increasing speculation. As its stock market value increased, everyone tried to outbid each other and its value increased even more, until it became worth more than twenty times the annual revenue of a highly skilled craftsman. This continued until the absurdity of the situation incited certain traders to leave the tulip market rather conspicuously, turning euphoria into panic, a pattern which was to repeat itself again and again. This crisis put an end to what the Dutch would later call *windhandel* (literally "wind trade") and the Dutch Republic proceeded to structure and regulate its financial markets. This then allowed them to entice capital from all over the world without arousing suspicion, and to invest that capital for themselves, then appropriating the majority of the profit from these savings to build a war and merchant fleet which would enable them to remain in power for another one hundred and fifty years.

In 1720, London was Amsterdam's most serious political, economic, and financial competitor, when the speculative bubbles of securities and currencies burst, causing the bankruptcy of the South Sea Company as well as some banks. The British government decided to structure and regulate the City, which enabled Britain to take power from the Dutch Republic in 1780, when many Dutch ship owners left Holland for London, which had become the safest and most dynamic city in Europe. The best financiers followed them. Eight years later, the main Dutch banks collapsed and the "heart" crossed the North Sea definitively to settle on the banks of the river Thames, where democracy and the economic market progressed as one. In 1844, a new financial crisis enabled the City to strengthen its position as the most powerful by using a central bank, and by imposing the gold standard for setting monetary parity.

Around 1890, the British Empire appeared triumphant, but in reality, was exhausted and accumulating debts, contracted to finance the defense of its colonies. The British Raj, in particular, was not earning as much as had been anticipated. The majority of British banks collapsed, as they had done half a century earlier. London would not withstand this time. Before the 20th century had begun, Boston had replaced London as the eighth "heart" of the world economy and Wall Street had replaced the City as the most powerful financial center.

Just as Amsterdam and London in the past, the American "heart," Boston, used the financial crisis of 1907 to strengthen its position. This crisis led to the creation of the Federal Reserve in Washington and gradually, the pound was replaced by the dollar in all international exchanges.

At this time, the nature of the world financial market changed once again. With the First World War looming, the banks that had been, for the majority, created in the 19th century (such as J.P. Morgan, Rockefeller, Chase, City, Lehman Brothers and Morgan Stanley), became receptacles for massive savings and stock investments, firstly with war bonds and then with shares and stock bonds. The capital markets became the main source of funds for businesses, which determined their corporate strategies according to their stock market values. "Insiders," informed before the rest of the existence of gold mines or oil reserves, or other money-making ventures, built huge fortunes with other people's savings.

The First World War quickened the industrialization of American mechanical production, Henry Ford had just launched factory assembly lines and this soon became the norm and salaries rose. New, totally uncontrolled forms of investments, such as holding companies and trusts, came into existence. American banks mixed deposit and investment activities and started to substitute themselves for British banks. They lent money generously in America, and the rest of the world, to those who were willing to buy property or securities. American capitalism seemed to be in an excellent state of health, except for the poorest people, notably African-Americans and Americans from the Appalachian region.

At the same time, a major crisis began, probably the most important historical one we have experienced until now. In order to understand what is happening today, we must reflect on what we can learn from this last crisis.

Firstly, from 1919 onwards, the wealthiest Americans saturated the property market in Florida. The upper-middle class also borrowed money in order to buy second homes; their loans were often secured by stock portfolios, the value of which increased with economic growth. At this time, optimism reached fever pitch, the most powerful country in the world felt itself blessed by God; America was happy.

In spring 1926, the demand for this particular type of property started to decline, but the prices continued to rise. This set the following chain of events (which we will see again later) into motion; misleading optimism, followed by banks advising ill-considered investments to customers who had placed all of their savings with the same bank, followed by a property bubble, followed by a bubble on the share market, which maintained the euphoria, consumer consumption and growth. All these factors contributed to widen the gap between rich and poor; in 1928, the richest 5% of the population appropriated more than a third of all American household income, which curbed the demand from the middle classes and threatened economic growth. So, the Federal state encouraged the American people to borrow more money to be able to consume, using the value of their shares as security. Consequently the price of shares kept climbing. As with any financial bubble, people were making their fortunes without working; the middle class spent more and more money that it did not have, contracting debts at great speed, but feeling reassured by the strength and growth of their stock portfolios. Optimism bordered on blindness. The financial system became very unstable. The situation was on the verge of turning from euphoria to panic at any moment.

Several events could have triggered the crisis. American banks had granted many loans abroad since The Great War, and they still had not been repaid. In 1928, the constitution of the Seven Sisters, a coalition of the biggest oil companies, increased the price of petrol and consequently reduced the demand for automobile production, but this was not interpreted as a sign of a forthcoming depression. Indeed, at the time, economists attributed this to the discontinuation of the Ford Model T, which had been replaced with a new model.

In late 1928, America's total debt (if we take all factors into account) was close to 300% and still nobody realized that the crisis had already started, even as, in the first six months of 1929, three hundred and forty five American banks closed! On October 20, huge profits and an increase in interest rates and margin calls caused stock market prices to drop. On the morning of Thursday October 24, stock market prices crashed (the Dow Jones was down – 22.5% by midday). Wall Street was bombarded by smaller investors wanting to sell off their shares. Institutional investors stepped in to support the stock market and at the end of the day, the share price index had only gone down 2.1% despite 12.9 million shares being sold; a colossal amount at the time. During the following days, the stock market crash worsened and caused financial ruin for those people who had used their stock portfolios to secure their loans. They sold everything in order to make their loan repayments and so the share price index continued to decrease. Panic spread to the banks; customers queued at the counters in order to salvage their savings, but the banks could not pay. In total, 4,000 banks went bankrupt that year, owing to lack of support.

An economic crisis followed the financial crisis; the construction and automobile industries were the first sectors concerned. In a few months, panic had spread all over the world. Each country looked for salvation in national protective measures, devaluing its currency to improve the competitiveness of its exports and reduce its trade gap. In 1931, Great Britain, wanting to keep the "imperial preference," suspended the convertibility of the pound to gold, and created the sterling area. Weimar's Germany, overcome by war debts and ruined by the crisis, brought in total control on exchanges. Japan suspended the convertibility of the yen to gold, and in turn, brought in general control of exchanges. The crisis deepened. Commercial exchanges became more and more restricted to exchanges within zones or countries using the same currency, transforming the American economic recession into a worldwide economic recession.

In March 1933, the new American president, Franklin D. Roosevelt, launched large-scale public works, suspending the convertibility of the dollar to gold, creating a dollar zone, and through the Glass Steagall act, asked banks to choose between the profession of investment bank or deposit bank; he forbade earnings on deposits in current accounts, and instructed the Federal Deposit Insurance Corporation to guarantee these deposits. Chase and City chose to become deposit banks. Lehman Brothers, Goldman Sachs and Morgan Stanley (founded by former J.P. Morgan employees) became investment banks.

Economic growth took off again, but weakly. In 1934, the United States devalued the dollar by 40% compared to gold. In 1936, Leon Blum's France abandoned, in turn, the convertibility of the franc to gold. In 1938, after a significant relapse of the American economy which proved the failure of Roosevelt's projects, he created a kind of public bank, Fannie Mae, to even out the risks in the housing sector. The growing unemployment reached 25% of the working population and national income went down by half. American banks started thinking about opening subsidiaries in London in order to do what was now forbidden in Wall Street.

The end of the financial and economic crisis that had begun twelve years earlier was signaled by the United States entering the Second World War. From October 1941, unemployment, which was still at 18% of the working population, started to go down. The Americans and the British started to consult each other about the post-war management of the world, in particular the monetary and financial organization. These negotiations lasted three years. The question of private banks and financial markets was not raised, even though they were largely responsible for the Great Depression, which was then only attributed to protectionism, devaluation and the orthodoxy of central banks. These secret negotiations were merciless: each time Washington gave military reinforcement to London, it was paid for with a political concession on the relationship between the pound and the dollar. De facto, war loans established the hegemony of the dollars that they were contracted in, without it being explicitly decided. The

British Treasury, with a debt that attained 250% of its GDP, was not in a position to negotiate.

At the very beginning of 1942, two opposing monetary reforms were put forward: the first by Harry Dexter White, deputy secretary of the U.S. Treasury and the second by the Englishman, John Maynard Keynes. They are worth discussing at length here, because their importance helps to understand the present financial situation and forthcoming debates.

White's program, "The Program for an Allied Monetary Fund," planned to create two institutions: allied funds to stabilize the exchange rate, and an allied bank whose function would be to help with the reconstruction and development of international commerce in countries which accept the setting up of liberal commercial and monetary strategies. He implied that the exchange standard could only be the dollar, with or without reference to gold. In "Propositions for an international Clearing Union," Keynes dared to write: "the ideal system would surely consist in the foundation of a supranational bank whose relationship with national central banks would be like those that exist between each central bank and subordinate banks." In his opinion, "this world central bank, with supranational status, will not only escape the gold standard but also the hegemony of a currency over the others, and should have all the attributes of a central bank with a supranational currency for payments between central banks. This bank of central banks, called the "Union," will manage accounts in "bancor," an international currency defined by comparison to gold. Member countries will receive "bancor" in exchange for their gold; the balances will be paid. If the overdrawn limit is exceeded, the member country can adjust its exchange rate in agreement with the Union and must make the necessary adjustments recommended by it."

His plan did not go down well in the United States. The Wall Street Journal described it as "a machine to regiment the world;" the American Bankers Association was very reserved about both propositions and suggested " a return to the gold standard, by far the best system imaginable," and declared that "a quota or share system in an international monetary pool, which would give debt-ridden countries the impression that they had a right to loans, is unhealthy in principle and would maintain unrealistic hopes."

In April 1942, White detailed his project: a "Stabilization Fund for the United and Associated Nations" to fix exchange rates and impose measures of realignment, and an "International Bank for Reconstruction and Development." Only the countries possessing gold assets could benefit from loans from the fund or the bank, in other words, first and foremost the United States. In reality, for White, the main purpose of the system was to limit America's obligations as a creditor, and to entitle it to use a blocking minority in both institutions when it came to important decisions, particularly loans. Keynes thought that the new version of White's plan did not allow international liquid assets to be adapted to world needs, and gave Americans too much power over other people's finances, but Great Britain did not have the strength to resist. In May 1942, Britain even had to sell her last stakes in the American arms industry to America in order to repay the annual installments on her loans. In May 1943, as the fate of the war seemed to be changing, White sent a questionnaire to forty-six country representatives in Washington; a month later, just before the American landing in Sicily, he held a "Technical Experts Meeting" attended by eighteen representatives of capital cities in Washington. In the fall, a meeting between British and American experts ended with a vague joint declaration.

In March 1944, the new Anglo-American consultation decided to organize a conference in Bretton Woods, a small town in New Hampshire. The British, hostile to negotiations that would take world financial control away from London and dethrone the pound in favor of the dollar, dragged things out, under the pretext that they had not yet consulted all Commonwealth member countries. This was in vain: on June 15, just one week after the Normandy landings, an editorial board, comprised of seventeen country representatives, met in Atlantic City to establish the agenda for the conference. The Americans reserved the positions of secretary and chairman and so presided over the Fund, as these were the only things that they were really interested in, and they named Keynes as president of the Bank commission.

On July 1, 1944, the conference began in Bretton Woods, in the presence of seven hundred delegates. The U.S. Secretary of the Treasury, Morgenthau was elected president, assisted by three vice-presidents who were Belgian, Brazilian and Russian. The official language was English. As planned, three commissions were created: the first, chaired by White, concentrated on the IMF. The second, chaired by Keynes, on the IBRD and the third, chaired by the Mexican, Suarez, studied other means of international financial cooperation. In his commission, Keynes led the debates at such speed that nobody could really keep up with him. On July 3, at the Funds commission, an American delegate deemed that a text detailing that the exchange rates would be stated in gold or a "currency convertible to gold at the date of 1, July 1944" was "insignificant." At this date, only the dollar was convertible; the text was approved without debate, but in fact it was the acceptance of the dollar-standard! On July 12, a British delegate went against Keynes' instructions and asked for the text to be modified. The phrase "currency convertible to gold" was changed to "currency convertible to gold or the U.S. dollar," which further confirmed the recognition of the dollar-standard. Keynes asked that this fundamental change be omitted in the ninety-six page document signed by the delegates, but it reappeared in the text that was sent out for approval by the different governments, written exclusively by the Americans! From that time on, everything was settled.

The debates on quotas, in other words on voting rights, were also very close. For France, Pierre Mendès France obtained a seat in each institution, but not the voting rights he asked for. On July 14, an agreement on the quotas was reached. China, Egypt, France, India, New Zealand and Iran expressed reservations.

On July 18, it was decided that the headquarters of the IMF and the IBRD would be in the United States. It was also decided that the Bank of International Settlements should be liquidated because of its participation in gold looting with the Nazis in Europe. This decision would not to be enforced. At the closing session of the conference, on July 22, 1944, Henry Morgenthau declared that these agreements would make it possible to "drive only the usurious money lenders out of the temple of international finance."

In fact, the system was warped from the beginning: the Bretton Woods agreements incited the United States to have an adverse balance of payments in order to provide the world with dollars, as dollars were the only form of payment recognized by these agreements. In the end, this could only serve to weaken confidence in this currency. In other words, the more the dollar became the reserve currency, the less trustworthy it would be. This paradox, otherwise known as the "Triffin dilemma," named after the Belgian-American economist who first developed it, is still totally relevant today, and has not yet reached its peak.

Yet, in the beginning, everything seemed to be going well: in 1945, the United States came out of the war, strongly convinced that they were in a dominant position. Its industrial production was double that of 1939. It produced half the coal, two thirds of oil, and over half the electricity in the world; and the majority of airplanes, cars, boats and weapons. It possessed 80% of the world gold reserves. Furthermore, the inequalities inside the United States had lessened: the richest 5% of the population only commanded 25% of the income, compared to 40% before the war.

The American financial system developed. In 1949, Alfred Winslow Jones created the first hedge fund using all the future financial speculative principles: leverage, forward selling, few investors, and management payments. Moreover, the American deposit banks, having low rates of return, started opening branches in London in order to get round the Glass Steagall Act. Despite the collapse of the British economy, the City became an annex of Wall Street. There, the financiers could perform in the same language the operations that were forbidden in the United States, starting with mixing the activities of investment and commercial banks.

Up until 1958, dollars remained rare outside of the United States. Then, the Vietnam War and the space race meant that America had to import machines and natural resources, thereby massively spreading dollars around the world. The countries that exported the most towards the United States accumulated huge dollar-reserves which gave way to an equivalent emission of their own currency, maintaining inflation, which some, like the Federal Republic of Germany absolutely did not want on any account. In 1965, Johnson's Equalization Tax created the Eurodollar market which did not incite dollars to be repatriated. On August 15, 1971, the government of Bonn asked for a refund of its dollars with gold, but the U.S. government, not wanting to see its gold reserves disappear, immediately suspended the convertibility of the dollar. This brings us back to the floating exchange rates between the two wars, that the Bretton Woods agreements were supposed to oppose. Confidence in the dollar was crumbling. This was followed by a very strong fall in the value of the American currency, which devalued the income of oil producing countries. Their reaction was the first oil crisis in October 1973, which set in motion the first major economic crisis since 1945. On December 9, 1974, Time magazine wrote "the nation is now also plunging deeper into a recession that seems sure to be the longest and could be the most severe since World War II."

On January 8, 1976, in Kingston, the Jamaica Agreements officially confirmed the end of the legal, international role of gold. In 1980, the United States, whilst still being in the middle of an economic crisis, seemed to be on the verge of a decline. Its currency collapsed and it lost its title as the top automobile exporter in the world. Its share of the world machine-tool market (25% in 1950) fell to 5% in 1980, whilst Japan, a new power, went from 0 to 22%. U.S. foreign debt massively increased, exceeding their assets abroad. Wall Street, victim of a serious financial crisis, was no longer the only place where the world's finance was organized; in London, (where a German emigrant, Sigmund Warburg, launched the first loans in eurodollars and the first takeover bid) the City seemed to be recuperating its position that had seemed forever lost. Japan became America's principal creditor and dramatically bought numerous token businesses and properties there. The American external deficit was getting deeper, and this encouraged a small number of central banks to bulk buy dollars; from then on, American public debt was the basis for most of the credit given out in the world. In thirty-five years, from 1945 to 1980, this basis was even multiplied by 200! Furthermore, in 1980, every dollar held by a bank at a central bank supported at least 40 dollars of credit in the U.S., and 50 in Europe, compared to only 15 and 20 in 1968! In 1980, the price of gold reached 800 dollars per ounce, the highest price in history. The productivity of America's biggest businesses was stagnant, and the country seemed to be nothing more than the breadbasket for a flourishing Japan. Technological innovations, in particular the microprocessor, were to overthrow this prognosis. These innovations were the basis of a large-scale public works program launched by Reagan under the name Star Wars, with a view to developing information technology (just as Roosevelt had done in 1933, when he launched a vast sanitation and electrical program). These innovations were to save the American "heart" which, instead of migrating from New York to Tokyo, turned to California (where these innovations were grouped together in Silicon Valley) without Wall Street losing its financial power. The rate of the dollar then tripled in three years compared to gold.

The strength of these innovations doubled every eighteen months, which would not only boost the productivity of the big American and international businesses and American economic growth, it would also disrupt the financial markets and start up the process that has led to today's financial crisis. The foreign exchange market, a source of many inventions thanks to the floating currencies, was soon to become just another one of the numerous channels used for cash to flow freely, without control, all over the world. This deregulation, particularly useful for the development of the Internet in Silicon Valley, was to eventually prove itself disastrous for the financial markets.

The first warning shot sounded in Wall Street on October 19, 1987. Following a significant American trade gap and a rise in the Federal Funds Rate at the Bundesbank, the Dow Jones lost 22.6% in one day and the other stock markets also fell that same day: it was the first stock market crash of the computer science era. On November 2, 1987, Time magazine's front cover read "The Crash: After a Wild Week on Wall Street, the World is Different." In 1988, the most important central banks met in Basel, and decided to adopt a ratio called "Cooke" which fixed the relationship between shareholders' equitycapital and the bank's liability at 8%. This is known as the Basel-I Accord.

In 1989, the fall of the Berlin Wall opened up a whole continent to commerce and the market economy, then others followed suit. Through the explosion of newly-industrialized countries in the early nineties, in particular China, who also adopted a market economy, globalization spread. This implied the globalization of the market, but not necessarily the rule of law.

So began a period of strong economic growth, the strongest in the history of humanity, along with a tremendous improvement in the standard of living for the middle classes in developing countries, and even a reduction of poverty. For the first time the number of people living on less than 2 dollars per day went down: from 1982 to 2002, their proportion went from 60% to 50% in Asia and from 44% to 30% in Latin America. On the other hand, in Africa, there was no decrease.

Progressively, the central banks started to transfer their power of regulation and currency issuing to the financial markets. Information technology enabled the expansion of credit and therefore of its counterpart, debt, through channels other than banks; all assets of all businesses contributed to this. Banks and other financial institutions became less and less transparent, keeping most of the profit they made, (with other people's money), for themselves. The globalization of finance preceded, accompanied and organized the globalization of trade, by allowing savings to be transferred quickly from the place where they were collected, that is to say, Europe or Asian oil-producing countries, to the place where they were used, mostly the U.S. Financial tools became more and more diverse (in particular with the RMBS, which will come up again) at the same time as interest rates were going down. Well informed financiers, or "insiders," were able to hope for significant returns through sharing risks with others.

Trade between the subsidiaries of the same company represented a growing share of international trade. Ultraliberal rules were established everywhere, under a new doctrine called the Washington Consensus. These rules advocated the freedom of the financial markets, the reduction of the state's role and the flexibility of work – the globalization of the stock market without the globalization of the rule of law.

Several bubbles formed and then burst one after the other, without having a real global or lasting effect. In 1991, in Sweden, there arose a financial crisis which everyone should have reflected upon: a property bubble sent the principal banks into semi-bankruptcy. They were nationalized by the government which then separated out the good debts from the bad and entrusted them to defeasance companies.

The situation of the good banks was restored and they were successfully privatized. At the same time, in the United States, the regulatory administration was gradually being broken up. In 1992, 20,000 civil servants were still employed by the "financial regulation." In 2008, there were only 14,000. In December 1994, Silicon Valley was booming with dotcom businesses, whilst just next door, Orange County lost 1.69 billion dollars speculating on the financial market, and so had to declare itself bankrupt. Following this unnecessary bankruptcy, (the risk for local government being very low), a very specific type of insurance, offering to insure local government loans, saw the day: these were monolines. Their insurance capacity was not founded on the capacity to finance a particular proportion of loss, but on a rigorous candidate selection, which, according to them, guaranteed that their clients could not default. They even claimed to be able to "insure" loans up to 150 times their capital value, without any opposition from regulators.

At the same time in 1992, the Maastricht Treaty enabled Europe to protect itself by introducing the euro and sharing out the risks.

In 1997, a brief and brutal Asian monetary and financial crisis spread, especially to Russia and Brazil. In September 1998, in the United States, an American hedge fund, LTCM, (which gambled on treasury bonds) was affected by mathematical (and other) mistakes made by its founding members, which caused significant debt; it was saved from collapsing only through the Fed's intervention. China was worried that the Asian crisis would lead to a reevaluation of its currency, and so started buying dollars. American economic growth and deficit were financed more and more by China's savings, a country which exported the majority of its industrial production to the United States. It was as if the world were managed by rather a strange couple made up of China and America, which Harvard University history professor, Niall Ferguson was to prettily name "Chimerica…"

Euphoria returned and deregulation accelerated. On November 12, 1999, the Financial Services Act eliminated the restrictions of the Glass Steagall Act, thereby legalizing retroactively the constitution of Citigroup, which had taken place the year before (grouping together Citicorp and Travelers Financial Group, which had gone back to investment banking through the merger with Salomon Smith Barney). So, the first American financial giant was created. Competition developed fiercely between banks, which invested up to twenty times their equitycapital. This American financial system evolution began to worry some people: in the same year, North Carolina forbade stockbrokers from using predatory lending. Still in 1999, a private company in Delaware developed new accounting norms, known as the IFRS. These advised asset evaluation at actual market value. The price of gold was only 300 dollars per ounce. Still in the same year, Japan lent the equivalent of 80 million dollars to banks on the verge of collapsing, with the understanding that this money would be reimbursed once the restructuring and merging of the bigger establishments had finished, and indeed it was. However, Japanese banks did not cancel their bad debts, therefore slowing down the reconstitution of their equitycapital.

In 2000, the Internet bubble, which had been growing for the past five years, burst; Nasdaq, which concentrated on technological values, went down by 27% in the first two weeks of April, and by 39.3% in the space of a year.

The warnings continued: the day after the 9/11 terrorist attacks in 2001, the Dow Jones went down 684 points (-7.3%), but that did not slow economic growth which was boosted by a sudden drop of interest rates. In 2002, the American energy stockbroker, Enron, forged its own accounts, and this, combined with the fraud of the American communications group, Worldcom, disrupted international stock markets and led to reforms that were to the advantage of the City, where many American banks were thriving. However, economic growth continued, nobody wanted to see the cracks forming. In order to dispense savings that they did not have, the banks reduced their reserves which only reached 0.2% of their deposits in 2001, as opposed to 11.3% in 1951!

The driving force of financial capitalism was appearing more clearly than ever to be greed. The wealthiest people, who could feel the crisis coming, continued to benefit from the situation as much as possible. The directors of financial businesses, especially those with access to the most precious information, the "insiders," who have no loyalty to anyone except themselves, shared a 10 billion dollar bonus in 2002! The market was more and more risky and so incited everyone to keep their cash. Even the least volatile assets were valued as if they were cash using valuation techniques called "mark to market" and "mark to model," set up by a corporate organization, The International Accounting Standards Board. Even though rules had been voted in Basel by the BIS in order to promote prudence and clarity, they were biased towards the strongest by imposing that all banks had ever-higher amounts of reserve funds.

In 2002, weak demand coupled with the avoidance of an income policy that would have been so contrary to traditional American politics, led the American government to encourage Freddie Mac and Fannie Mae, and other housing protagonists to allow less creditworthy borrowers take on high risk products, subprimes, which provided a better interest rate.

World economic growth started up again, nourished by the indebtedness of all the protagonists of the economy, and supported by the drop of interest rates.

Few are those who, like Professor Maurice Allais in Paris and the eccentric and unconventional Professor Hyman Minsky in New York, (admired by Marxists and Hedge Fund managers), announced the oncoming of a serious financial crisis. Minsky imagined the crisis as having five phases: profitable development, (or a change of economic policy), a boom, euphoria, profits, and finally a moment of panic which has been nicknamed "the Minsky moment" and that he foresaw for 2009…

CHAPTER 2

HOW IT ALL BEGAN

The preceding financial crises were, as previously stated, either the time to question the economic system of the moment, or an occasion to test its strength. In both cases, they are indicative of human incapacity to have access to perfect information about the future. Couldn't the crisis starting so mysteriously today be a mere setback just like the other crises that have happened since 1980? Or could it be a long crisis, that only a world war will put an end to, like in 1929? Or perhaps a long, troubled transitional period, moving towards a technological jolt, like the crisis that lasted from 1971 to 1982? A new sort of speculative bubble bursting, like the tulip bubble in 1637, that then contributed to Amsterdam's hegemony? Or, on the contrary, a profound crisis of a tired financial system like the crisis of 1880, which was the beginning of the decline of Great Britain?

In my opinion, it is effectively a youthful crisis: it is the first crisis since globalization began, and it could, just like the tulip crisis, announce the start of a tremendous period of economic growth. But for that to be the case, we must understand it and learn from it. For that, we must dissect its daily development, using the simplest possible terms, to understand how, after so many limited crises, the Great Crisis of today, the oncoming of which everybody turned a blind eye to, began.

The crisis started in the United States, and for the first time, thanks to the Internet, insurance companies, investment funds and investment banks, has literally become a planetary crisis. The crisis whose start looks a lot like its ancestor of 1929, but with a much greater magnitude.

Insufficient Demand

Everything began with the liberalization of the economy, without any democratic counterbalance, which led to an increase in the profit share of national income everywhere in the world. In particular, the profit made in the financial sector, where the "insiders" could keep most of the income for themselves: whereas in 1960 their earnings represented 14% of the profits made by all American businesses, in 2008, they represented 39%. All of the newly created wealth was therefore increasingly monopolized by a small group of people claiming a 20%

return on the capital that they invested, mostly by borrowing at lower and lower interest rates. This led to a situation of growing income inequality: the richest 1% of the American population earned more than 16% of the national income, compared to 7% in 1948; 5% of the American population allocated themselves 38% of the income and half the holdings created between 1990 and 2006. This went hand in hand with a more and more dominant political influence. Nobody wanted to admit that an economic growth of 5% per year cannot guarantee a 20% increase in incomes for any length of time.

Consequently, the relative value of salaries went down: even though American economic growth had been at 4% since 1990, the average American salary was stagnant. The average salary of an American citizen today is even lower than that of 1979; for the poorest 20% it is even much lower. The least rich 50% can claim only 2.8% of holdings. From 1947 to 1973, the income of the poorest fifth of the American population (all sources of income combined) grew by 116%, which is a lot more than any other group of the population. Up until 2004, it only grew by 2.8%, which is a lot less than the growth of debt within this same group.

The same thing happened in other countries. In twenty years in France, the share index has increased by 120%, whilst salaries (for full time workers) have only increased by 15%, and the national minimum wage has not increased at all.

In the end, this transfer of wealth weighs on demand: through insufficient salaries, the American and European middle class cannot consume as much as before. Furthermore, the ageing of the population (which immigration has hardly slowed down in the United States) is also affecting demand, as it decreases for each individual, on average, after 50 years of age.

Debt-Created Demand

In the United States, in order to preserve economic growth without questioning the distribution of wealth, it was necessary to maintain demand without increasing salaries, in other words, to incite the middle classes to get into debt: this is what American society tacitly decided to do in the 1980s with the introduction of credit cards for every day consumables, and through mortgage loans. Consumer credit (used for everyday life, and also for cars, education, healthcare and holidays) was promoted through saturation advertising: on average, an American household received one new credit card offer every week in the mail! Credit companies and political authorities, including President Bush, encouraged households to go further into debt, they only asked for a monthly repayment of 2-3% of the balance owed. Nearly a third of American households accumulated 10,000 dollars of debt on their credit cards. The system quickly became overpowering. The interest rates for these debts were often between 11% and 15%, but in the case of a late repayment, they could jump to 29% or 34%.

Mortgage credit is quite as strategic on economic and political planes, in particularly for minority communities: in the United States, everybody owns their own home, or has the right to become a homeowner. In 1977, the Community Reinvestment Act encouraged banks and building societies to lend to disadvantaged communities. These financial institutions, having been close to bankruptcy around 1980, hesitated about lending to these not very creditworthy clients, pressure groups from various communities then launched campaigns and obstructed mergers between the banks that failed to fulfill their commitments to housing projects. Consequently, mortgages with different levels of loan qualities were developed, according to the borrower's profile.

Independent brokers, paid through bonus systems, offered borrowers with the worst repayment history, subprime mortgages with graduated interest rates, but the amount of the loan was sometimes more than the value of the house, and the final total could be more than thirty times their annual income. As these mortgages were asset-based, guaranteed by the value of the house, everybody could borrow more, as long as property prices continued to rise. And they did rise! The system was without risk for the banks. Freddie Mac and Fannie Mae, the partly public institutions created after the Great

Depression, bought these contracts from the banks, encouraged by the Congress.

Intermediary loans, called Alt-A loans, which are between prime loans and subprime loans, were offered to the less poverty-stricken, with no partial or even total interest repayment for the first years.

A lot of people contended that these loans maintained economic growth, by inciting property building, and in the process, releasing income through which more property and products could be consumed. The economy of debt was of use to the government, banks, industries and employees. In fact, the property market and the financial services, which nourished each other, represented 40% of economic growth in the American private sector. In Britain, where the same systems were set up by the same banks, it was 50%. There was, therefore, economic growth, but only in the sectors directly related to this activity. Young graduates drifted towards these jobs. On the other hand, research posts and engineering jobs were less and less prized.

Just like households, businesses also went into debt through riskier and riskier means. Directors and financiers bought out these businesses with little capital and large loans with very low interest rates, by imposing returns of the order of 20% from the purchased business. These returns were often superior to what the business would normally earn in order to allow the reimbursement of the loans taken out to buy the businesses thanks to the profits they made. Special private equity and LBO funds were established to attract savings towards these operations which were particularly profitable for their promoters. In order to attain such high returns, the businesses were encouraged to reduce their field of activity so as to concentrate on only the core activities corresponding to their particular knowledge. Employment was the first victim. Research was the second. The survival of the firms was the third.

The Drop in Interest Rates, Leverage and Wealth Effect

In order for the development of household and business debt to become tolerable, interest rates needed to drop, as was decided by the Fed from 2001 onwards. This was a key decision made by Mr. Greenspan, and it was welcomed by all, but it turned out to be a disaster. In fact, this decision allowed businesses, investment funds, and private individuals to borrow more. This "wealth effect" allowed indebted households to contract even more debt and to consume more, which pushed property prices to rise again. This was not just an American phenomenon; at the beginning of the 21st century, the value of property worldwide (which was increasing for demographic reasons) was estimated at 75T[3], in other words, one and a half times the world GDP,

---

[3] T: trillion.

whereas ten years earlier, it had been under three quarters of the world GDP.

In the same way, the value of businesses rose, calculated as a multiple of the profits. Firstly because, as previously stated, the share of profits within the national income rose; then because the expectancy of a rise in profits increases this multiple itself, which could from then on, attain eighty times the profits. The value of all the world's bonds and shares, equal to its GDP in 1980, was estimated at 100T mid-2006, in other words, double the value of the world GDP; to which we should add (as we will see) outstanding shares and derivative products from the world over, which, according to some serious estimations could exceed 70 to 100T. In total, the global, financial and real-estate assets were estimated at more than 250T, mostly financed by debt. A mountain of irresponsible debt! Everything was set up for an avalanche to start.

*Frantic Pursuit of Savings: Securitization
and Derivative Products*

The ageing of the population pushes for higher returns: senior citizens, (particularly in the United States), must build up a pension plan that lasts longer and longer by pursuing the highest returns.

From early 2000 onwards, in order to obtain more financing, which is the raw material for their work and the source of their profits, banks did everything they could to make these mortgage loans attractive for institutional savers all over the world, in particular offshore hedge funds, so as not to keep the most risky loans on their balance sheets.

The banks split up the riskiest loans, particularly subprimes, according to their level of risk, then regrouped them in batches: RMBS (residential mortgage backed securities), equity (the riskiest), that certain traders called "loss money," mezzanines (intermediary), seniors, and even the super-seniors (AAA). These "batches" were then resold as bonds on the stock market. This is what is called "securitization" (which has been made possible by new technology, mathematical models and the Internet.) This operation quickly became a big success, thanks to the returns promised to the buyers of these bonds. All the institutional savers in the world wanted some of these securitized products, subprimes and the rest, for themselves, or to place them for their clients. The amount of these bonds, real estate or otherwise, quickly exceeded 12T, in other words, it exceeded the amount of American treasury bonds. Freddie Mac and Fannie Mae followed suit and kept some mortgage loans on their balance sheets, but sold others as RMBS. Half of these subprime bonds were sold to non-American banks, which sold the other half to their non-American clients.

This success encouraged the development of all kinds of debt to be sold as bonds under the name "asset-backed securities." Certain securitized bonds, intended for private individuals, (CDOs: collateralized debt obligations) particularly credit card debts developed rapidly. Certain CDOs included subprime RMBS parts. All promised returns by far superior to economic growth. All these bonds were fundamentally useful in the beginning, and this could have continued, on two conditions; firstly that the savers understood what they were buying, and secondly that securitization did not become an excuse to offer borrowers loans that were impossible to reimburse.

Financial derivatives were also securitized. A little technical explanation is necessary here, even though skipping these details is of no consequence.

Derivatives are financial instruments that appeared to insure oneself against the risk of the shifting value of "underlying" assets (shares, bonds, loans or even interest and exchange rates.) They are useful in rendering the circulation of savings sounder and safer. The value of these derivatives "derives" from the assets they depend on. This is where their name comes from. Derivatives constitute bets on the evolution of these assets; four main types of derivative exist, according to the nature of the bet: futures, forwards, options and swaps. In particular, there are two main categories of derivatives based on debts: the derivatives that are not based on assets, (a simple contract by mutual agreement, like, as we will see, the CDS), and derivative stocks linked to assets (like CDOs, based on securities of numerous assets.)

These derivatives are securitized; therefore in CDOs, there are several blocks of derivatives which are more or less profitable according to the risk taken by the buyers. The valuation mechanism of these securitized products relied on the evolution of more and more complicated formulae, which was less and less comprehensible to the bank managers offering these products. Certain financial establishments offered their clients the possibility to invest their savings in securities of this sort, but the product description came in a one hundred and fifty page manual that even a top bank executive could not understand or control.

These diverse securitized and/or derivative products, promised exceptional returns and so were sold, amongst other financial products, by investment banks (Bear Stearns, Merrill Lynch, Citigroup, Lehman Brothers, AIG) and by hedge funds to all financial institutions in around the world, which were impatient to benefit from this new godsend, and to invent the same type of products themselves without anyone ever being able to trace back to their origin. If, within some banks and hedge funds, certain individuals knew a little about the risks being taken, (but without that affecting their hunger for profit), individual savers, at the other end of the chain, had no way of understanding them. The asymmetry of information was of an unequalled scale. This is the true cause of this crisis.

All possible, imaginable stocks could be adapted to all sorts of savers and were mixed up within the outstanding global derivative products, the total of which exceeded 12T. New accounting standards meant that banks had to evaluate these products on their balance sheets, without using the stock market, according to a mathematical model which fixed an ever-changing theoretical value. Everything became virtual; income and assets.

The directors of these financial businesses and the creators of these products were paid mainly with bonuses linked to the annual profit that they made. Unlike the employees, they shared in the profits; but unlike the shareholders, they did not share in the losses.

So, savings came from everywhere, from Europe, oil-producing countries and China to benefit from this new El Dorado. This created a higher demand for places to hide from taxation authorities, these being offshore centers; where the most respectable banks established "vehicles" that they turned a blind eye to. Four hundred banks could be found in offshore centers, in fact two thirds of two thousand hedge funds and two million shell corporations represented 10T of financial assets and derivatives.

No central bank, nor stock market authority, nor the IMF, nor the BIS found anything to say about it.

Insurers Create CDSs and Monolines
to Overcome the Difficulty of Attracting Capital

The crisis started. Nobody saw it coming, but it had set itself in motion: savers the world over were reluctant to buy financial products that were more and more unfamiliar. They understood that investment funds minimized the capital that they invested to get maximum leverage, and that if the financial instrument was no longer profitable, it would be them, the lenders, who would be the last resort payers. Given the reticence of the lenders, and to avoid increasing interest rates, which would reduce profit margins, banks and other financial institutions started to borrow not only on each financial operation, but also from their balance sheets, which supposedly shared out the risks. So as these products could not be seen on their balance sheets, the banks hid them in "specialized vehicles," in exotic locations which allowed them to conceal them from regulators. From 2004-2006 in Basel, central bankers established, new, more careful regulations, called Basel-II. This reform intensified the rules for internal control and clarity, but only for banks in developed countries.

Certain financial institutions offered to guarantee their hesitant lender's investments against risks, in asset-backed securities. This marked the surreptitious entrance of another major player to the stock market: the insurer, in the form of bankers, hedge fund managers, brokers or traditional insurers. These were sophisticated insurers, too sophisticated even, who invented discreet instruments to diffuse, dilute, and mask the risks of these products from savers.

Firstly, there was the CDS (credit default swap), a private pseudo-insurance contracted by mutual agreement between two parties, without any regulation, whereby the seller, a self-proclaimed insurer, insures the buyer of the CDS that he will reimburse any losses that he may incur due to a third party defaulting, in exchange for an annual bonus (or over several years) fixed according to the risk of loss as interpreted by these two parties. In particular, these CDSs allow savers to buy securitized products, whilst at the same time insuring themselves against the risk of insolvency on the part of the issuing companies. Therefore, these situations appear to be without risk. However, market protagonists are incorrigible gamblers and as always, an excellent financial instrument can be misappropriated from its purpose: the CDSs quickly became a simple "bet" that did not insure anything. Worse still, the CDSs were also securitized and transformed into stock market gambles. Their movement was so great and so successful that today, in the balance sheets of their owners, they account for 62T, which measures the history of their movements, but not their final value. Nobody knows who insures what anymore, nor for how much… Nobody knows the real value of these products.

At the same time, other insurers, monolines, came into being (FGIC, MBIA, Ambac and SCA). As we have already seen, these financial institutions were especially created to insure local governments. From 2004 onwards, monolines diversified and started to include securitized products: they reinsured, with only a signature, loan applications that were no longer guaranteed by local governments (which represented a large number of households and businesses), but by private individual borrowers. In this way, monolines claimed to insure 2.4T of securities, even though they absolutely did not guarantee the lenders against the risks they said they would because they did not have the necessary funds available. However, nobody, no regulator, government, central bank, (not even Mr. Greenspan at the Fed) or credit rater wanted to see it!

The Blindness of Credit Rating Agencies

In theory, credit rating agencies are supposed to be independent and incorruptible institutions, which come to visit businesses in order to tell savers and investors what to think of their management, their financial strength and their clarity. The agency awards a grade, from which the interest rate, that must be paid by the business in order to obtain a loan, is fixed. One could imagine that this position would be filled by a state-run company, or by international agencies, or at least by a non-profit organization. Today, this is done by private companies, and in particular by three companies: S&P, Moody's and Fitch. They are paid by the businesses themselves for giving them their grade! It is in the best interest of these agencies to do their job as rigorously as possible in order to maintain their reputation and their image. However, it is also in their interest not to displease their customers, who could turn to another agency if they find their grade unfair or insufficient.

This is what happened: as all the other protagonists in this story, the credit rating agencies, hoping to make the most money possible out of their clients, and wanting their share of this new wealth that had appeared out of nowhere, awarded grades with guilty indulgence. They did not even visit all of the businesses and see all of the products, from RMBS to CDOs and CDSs: how could they be critical of clients who bring in so much money? In fact, the total income of the three main agencies doubled between 2002 and 2007, going from 3 to 6 billion dollars. Moody's profits even quadrupled between 2000 and 2007! For five consecutive years, Moody's profit margin exceeded those of the five hundred biggest businesses analyzed by Fortune magazine and these were businesses that Moody's was supposed to rate...

The Explosion of Global Debt

With this general connivance, debts could do nothing but explode: at the end ofin 2007, Americans had accumulated 900 billion dollars of private debt on bank cards, double that the amount of ten years before. American household debt went from 46% of the GDP in 1979 to 98% in December 2007. American external debt reached more than 7T, in other words, 70% of the GDP. In 2007, that debt alone equaled 165 billion dollars, double what it was in 2002. The total combined American debt reached 350% of the GDP in December 2007, more than in 1929. In Great Britain, where salaries had been decreasing for ten years whilst household debt had been rising, the same thing occurred. In thirty years, British external debt went from 20% to 80% of the GDP. The same thing happened in France and elsewhere, at least where public debt is concerned. Only a few rare countries, like Canada and Chile, had reduced their debt before 2008. Leverage effect generates debt. Nobody can reimburse it. The avalanche was looming. The crisis had arrived. However, only a few could see it as yet.

Those Wwho Hhad Foreseen the Crisis

Mr. Paulson, as American minister of finance, (and previously president of Goldman Sachs, as was his predecessor Mr. Rubin in the Clinton era), should have known better than anybody, but knew nothing and saw nothing. Just as the IMF, at the time directed by a Spaniard, Mr. Rato. All European ministers of finance repeated that nothing could justify the pessimism of certain people: and they insisted that the "American decline" had been wrongly predicted for thirty years.

Yet, numerous experts had long believed that American public debt would soon become unmanageable, and were expecting the dollar and the American economy to crash. August 18, 2004, Martin Wolf, chief economics commentator at the Financial Times, explained that "America (is) on the comfortable path to ruin." December 21, 2004, Nouriel Roubini, an economics professor at New York University, (who just two years later was to become a guru whose words were worth gold), predicted that the dollar would crash in 2005, or 2006 at the latest. Others predicted an economic slowdown caused by the rise in the price of raw materials and staple foods.

Very few experts actually distinguished that it was private, not public debt that was going to cause the problem. Even fewer experts understood that the crisis was going to be triggered by real estate debt coming from the poorest households. Yet, some experts guessed that this was the case.

Belgian anthropologist, Paul Jorion, who became a Californian banker and who wrote one of the very first books announcing the crisis, recalled: "It was in 2003 that my colleagues and I at Wells Fargo (an investment bank) started discussing a forthcoming crisis."

In September 2004, Andy Xie, the chief economist at Morgan Stanley Asia, was the first to go public. At the Morgan Stanley Global Economic Forum, he explained that an overproduction was brewing and that it would have already caused deflation if the Fed had not artificially created currency by letting a real estate bubble form. He said that this bubble was just putting off an inevitable realignment, which would only become more severe. In his opinion, fighting deflation, which was then only just beginning, with bubbles would only put off and worsen deflation.

September 10, 2005, Raghuram Rajan, director of research at the Graduate School of Business at the University of Chicago, wrote that the creation of a big number of intermediaries increased the financial system's capacity to take risks, but let major threats hang over the principal world equilibrium.

September 7, 2006, at an IMF meeting, Nouriel Roubini spoke about the risks linked to the increase in the price of oil and interest rates, after which he explained "in the months and years to come, the United States risks seeing a serious recession." This would be caused by the madness of homeowners using their houses like cash machines (borrowing against the value of their houses), and the greed of financial institutions, which securitize mortgage loans, which in turn risks paralyzing the financial system. He announced the forthcoming collapse of hedge funds, investment banks, and other major financial institutions such as Freddie Mac and Fannie Mae. This speech soon made him into a guru; each of his words were to be dissected and used as a stock market reference.

September 11, 2006, in Paris, Nassim Nicholas Taleb, a former trader who was to publish a book in New York that was to become hugely successful, *the Black Swan,* about crisis theories, sparked off a scandal by calling Harry Markowitz, who invented the mathematical theory that founded portfolio management, a charlatan. In his book, he wrote: "Fannie Mae, (when I look at its risks,) seems to be sitting on a barrel of dynamite." The rare investors who listened to him made a fortune speculating on the real estate market decline. This was how Paulson and Co. funds made 3.7 billion profit in 2007 by speculating on the onset of the crisis.

Why Didn't We Listen to Them?

Indeed, all those who then still had the power to halt this drift, had everything to gain from letting it continue. Politicians, because economic growth satisfies voters. Borrowers, because it allows them to buy houses beyond their means. Bankers, credit raters, intermediaries and monolines because they deduct huge commissions in the process, out of all proportion to the wealth created. The only party with anything to lose is the future. This is quite normal as the future has no say in what is happening now. In order to stop these rare but worrying speeches from spreading, a theory or a thought process, or a dogma was invented: positive attitude. This consists of persuading oneself that any goal can easily be attained if we aspire to it with enough sincerity, strength and concentration. The conviction that, come what may, the outcome will be the best if we really believe it, has spread by and large throughout the world to the economy, sport and art. In the country where anything and everything has been possible for two centuries, this thirst for the power of words over reality became an ideology.

Protestant America, which started with Calvinism, promoting work and savings, thus came to cultivate the idea that God chose it and guarantees its victory. The theory of sufficient grace thus came to feed the positive attitude.

Everybody started to believe that being optimistic was a recipe for finding a good job. In particular, and this is an important point, it is impossible to become a director if you announce possible disasters. Just as taking on the financial responsibility of a variable rate mortgage all comes down to being able to persuade ourselves that we have the means to pay it. On the financial shelves of American and then European bookshops, most of the periodicals were dedicated to the advantages of positive thinking. They warned directors against the dangers of mistaking realism with pessimism. Several American businesses even employed specialized gurus to help them elaborate procedures institutionalizing optimism, by promoting cheerful speeches and events within the company, such as exotic holidays and dream cruises for executives. The least optimistic people had to go through counseling sessions so as to be rehabilitated. These types of gurus proudly published their lists of the most optimistic clients, including the directors of Lehman Brothers and Merrill Lynch!

At this time everything was going well with the economy, in particular in California, and as American technical feats on the Internet continued to change the world, nobody could see that an essential part of talent and capital was being embezzled by the financial system to the disadvantage of industry and research. It was very difficult to leave the table part way through the feast.

Everything carried on as if it were a ball where everybody only wants to see the sumptuous buffet and the magnificent orchestra, without realizing that there was only one exit. Everybody believed that there could not be problems. Those who understood that there could be some risks continued dancing, but given that the room was crowded, they stayed near the door.

Let's take another image. Everything was carrying on, just like robbers during a hold-up who hesitate to leave the safe room, knowing that the police are on their way but they think that nothing can happen to them.

Finance and Cocaine

Another apparently unrelated factor could have played a significant role: cocaine. All around the world, an increasing number of people, especially among the very young, are becoming addicted to cocaine, a much greater number than cowardly adults will admit to. Even if the price per dose is falling, this industry's turnover is fast-growing and rivals that of the world's largest companies: amounting to 100 billion dollars, for an estimated annual production of only 1,000 tons.

Cocaine arrived in Europe over five centuries, and is particularly adapted to those searching to escape the constraints of reality, allowing them to dare to do what their sense of ill-being or their reason inhibits them from doing, especially in an intensely competitive world.

A cocaine addict develops a virtual mind, which must be fed more and more every day, eating away at his real mind. In little time, he no longer perceives any moral constraints, he no longer has a Rule of Law, and he no longer sets limits or is able to apply restraint. He thinks he has absolute intelligence and that he is able to solve all problems. He also thinks he is indifferent to pain, fatigue, sleep and hunger. He thinks he is invincible and is convinced his judgment is infallible.

The world of finance is the reflection of this world without a Rule of Law, where anything is possible, in an optimistic and virtually absolute environment; it is a highly competitive world spread over all international markets, awake and active 24/7. Therefore, it is the perfect environment for cocaine addicts, euphoric sleepwalkers, to be themselves: it is not surprising that there are so many of them on trading room floors, nor is the amount of risks they have taken surprising.

The cocaine-addicted trader never doubts his own decisions, decisions that become more and more erratic; he prevails on absurd investments then sinks into pessimism, depression, paranoia and finally panic. This is exactly what has happened on the markets, foreshadowing what could be a world in the clutches of cocaine: a euphorically unreal, unconscious and suicidal nightmare.

Another factor, seemingly with no rapport, could have played a significant role: cocaine. All around the world, an increasing amount of people are becoming addicted to cocaine, especially among the very young, a high greater amount than cowardly adults will admit to. Even if the price per dose is falling, this industry's turnover is fast-growing and rivals that of the world's largest companies: amounting to 100 billion dollars, for only an estimated 1,000 tons of annual production.

Present in Europe for over five centuries, cocaine is particularly adapted to those searching to escape the constraints of reality to dare to do what their ill being or their reason inhibits them from doing, especially in an intensely competitive world.

A cocaine addict develops a virtual mind, which must be fed more and more every day, downhill euphoric phases, withering away his real mind. In little time, he no longer perceives any moral constraints, he no longer has a Rule of Law, and he no longer sets limits or is able to put on his brakes. He thinks he has absolute intelligence and that he is able to solve all problems. He also thinks he is indifferent to pain, fatigue, sleep and hunger. He thinks he is invincible and is convinced his judgment is infallible.

The world of finance is the reflection of this world without a Rule of Law, where anything is possible, in an optimistic and virtually absolute environment; it is a highly competitive world spread over all international markets, awake and active 24/7. Therefore, it is the perfect environment for cocaine addicts, euphoric sleepwalkers, to be themselves: it is not surprising that there are so many of them on the trading room floors, nor is it surprising the amount of risks they have taken.

The cocaine-addicted trader never doubts his own decisions, decisions which become more and more erratic; He prevails on absurd investments, then sinks into pessimism, depression, paranoia then panic. Exactly what has happened on the markets, foreshadowing what could be a world in the clutches of cocaine: a euphorically unreal, unconscious and suicidal nightmare.

The Reversal of the Subprime Market – .
The Economy of Panic.

Yet, the crisis has arrived. From the first quarter 2005 onwards, new building projects of accommodation decreased in the United States and by the third quarter, sales had slowed down. During the fourth quarter, the rise of real estate prices had slowed down. House prices started to decrease. Securitized products were designated as being "toxic," when it became clear that the residual value owed to the bank was superior to the actual value of the property. During the first quarter 2006, the number of payment defaults by subprime borrowers increased; in August 2006, a first mortgage institution, that markets them, went bankrupt. However, these loans continued: in 2006, one in four new mortgage loans was a subprime.

Moreover, the payment defaults did not only concern the subprime loans: in 2006, the financial press agency, Bloomberg, estimated that 16% of payments over two months late were for Alt-A loans, normally used for better quality housing, and 14% of Americans said that they were finding it difficult to keep up with their repayments.

This became a heavily indebted society. Borrowers who could no longer repay their debts… In general, this would be the chosen moment for governments to proclaim that there was no problem. More clear-headed citizens concluded that there was a catastrophe waiting just around the corner. Through thinking about it, they precipitated it by selling off their assets in order to keep the cash.

This is where the chain of events started: as in each crisis, fear turned to panic which triggered a stampede of people trying to "get out," but with some casualties along the way. Panic is completely different from fear; it leads to unpredictable change. Fear is also cleverly orchestrated by those whose interest it is to let us believe that the world will collapse if they are no longer paid their bonuses indexed to profits and stock market prices.

In order to understand the chain of events that led to today's situation, from now on we must study events day by day, until President Obama came into power, but only concentrating on those which have a direct link with the crisis.

Chronology

In February 2007, when everyone was worried about the effect of economic growth on the price of staple foods and oil, new accounting regulations imposed the valuation of assets on the stock market price. Banks then realized that they had not really got rid of the assets they had securitized, and for legal reasons, these assets could reappear on their balance sheets. This made them worry about their obligation to account for them. The Basel Accords forced them to insure that their loans depended on their shareholder equitycapital, and the lower valuation of their capital shareholder equity meant that they could go bankrupt. The trap set up by the Basel Accords and the IFRS (two informal institutions) was closing in on the banks.

In June 2007, the investment bank Bear Stearns announced the bankruptcy of two hedge funds that had invested in subprimes. In July, when two million Americans could no longer repay their mortgages and were forced to sell their houses, Wynne Godley, from the Levy Institute explained that: "American household debt is intolerable." Bill White, a BIS economist in Basel, was just as worried, but did not speak out in public. In August, the American real estate decline meant that there were more subprime borrowers who defaulted on their mortgages. The properties were repossessed and sold, which accelerated the fall in the prices of assets and associated securitized products.

Then one incident triggered the realization that this crisis was not just American and that the securitized subprimes could be found all over the world, and could not be traced. August 10, according to Paul Jorion: "It was a French bank, BNP Paribas, which sounded the alarm bell." People started to understand that this did not just concern a few poor American borrowers. It also became apparent that some European banks were even more fragile than the Americans because their shareholder equitycapital was lower: whilst in the United

States the banks lend 96 cents for every dollar deposited, the European banks lend 1.4 euros for every euro deposited! Even though the European banks do this whilst taking less risks, banks that were thought to be solid turned out to be affected, through lack of equitycapital. September 13, 2007, Northern Rock, the fifth largest British bank, asked the Bank of England for emergency help. It was a "young," provincial bank (founded in 1965 in Newcastle, it first floated on the London Stock Exchange in 1997), specialized in mortgage loans with low interest rates and relatively high risks (comparable to the American Alt-A loans, in other words, slightly less risky than subprimes). Northern Rock needed constant re-financing, which was more and more difficult to obtain, and was very late in asking the Bank of England to guarantee its loans. This did not stop a 72% fall of its stock market value, as well as queues in front of all its branches, which worsened its liquidity crisis.

On September 13, in New York, Nouriel Roubini, who was listened to more and more attentively, repeated that: "for as long as homes are used as personal cash dispensers, private consumption will continue to rise with no real foundation." On September 14, the Bank of England granted an emergency loan to Northern Rock to prevent it from going bankrupt.

The governor of the Bank of England was hesitant: was it necessary to help the banks? The new president of the Fed, Ben Bernanke, did not dawdle: he had written his thesis on the crisis of 1929, and was convinced that the role of a central bank was to help the citizens of its country, and was persuaded that for Americans, what counts more than anything else is economic growth, and so was determined not to let recession set in; but how far would he go? He hesitated about opening the floodgates of currency issuing. As far as Jean-Claude Trichet, president of the ECB, was concerned, he did not back down, even though he was in charge of making the euro into an internationally recognized reserve currency. To the horror of his colleagues, he agreed to increase the number of assets deposited at the central bank in exchange for currency issuing in favor of banks claiming, albeit discreetly, to be in difficulty. Through these actions, he saved the world financial system, and the Fed was persuaded into doing the same thing.

On October 1, UBS and Citigroup announced important asset depreciation linked to subprime and derived products. Several other European and American banks made similar announcements in the following days. The central banks helped them through. On October 8, a UBS economist, George Magnus wrote in the Financial Times that: "Bank liquidity is threatened. The debt reduction process is only just beginning."

In December 2007, the ex-president of the Fed, Alan Greenspan, still without remorse about the decisions he had made, and convinced that the reduction in interest rates was necessary, considered that the ensuing bubble was "the most recent demonstration of the human disposition for euphoria," of which he quoted another example with the "tulipmania in Holland in the XVIIth century."

In January 2008, many American banks, like Freddie Mac and Fannie Mae owed their solvency only to loans from the Fed and sovereign funds from Emirates, Singapore and China. On January 22, the Fed dropped its intervention rate by three quarters of a point to 3.5%, a measure of an exceptional scale. By the end of the month, the stock markets were doing better. Nevertheless, Paul Jorion announced threats for Credit Agricole, Caisse d'Epargne, Natixis... All the while, Roubini continued to insist that we'd seen nothing yet!

In fact, we'd seen nothing yet: On February 7, in London, Northern Rock was nationalized. On March 4, in Wall Street, the investment bank, Bear Stearns nearly went bankrupt, abandoning 13,400 billion dollars of transactions on derivative products, which was a lot more than Long Term Capital Management (LTCM) in 1998. 13.4T: a staggering figure, which exceeded the GDP of the country.

On March 11, for the first time since 1929, the Fed decided to allow investment banks, including Bear Stearns, to apply for refinancing, which is normally reserved for deposit banks. It was an incredible decision: the Fed does not control investment banks, which are under the supervision of the SEC, but was ready to support them without having seen the contents of their balance sheets! On March 14, J.P. Morgan and the Fed allocated a loan to Bear Stearns to prevent it from going bankrupt. March 16, J.P. Morgan Chase bought out Bear Stearns for 2 dollars per share (as opposed to 93 dollars in February) thanks to a 29 billion Treasury loan that was not guaranteed by anything. The stock market applauded the taxpayers' arrival in the financing of its mistakes. The next day, Jim Reid, an analyst at Deutsche Bank, wrote: "The United States is moving comfortably towards ruin. The longer the process takes, the harder the shock on the dollar and the standard of living will be."

On March 24, under the threat of legal action, J.P. Morgan upped the Bear Stearns offer to 10 dollars per share, 1.2 billion dollars in total. Where was the money to be found? In April, Nouriel Roubini, whose words were now conditioning the behavior of investors, wrote: "I foresee a serious liquidity crisis, which will lead to the breakdown of the financial system on an unprecedented scale. The federal government must intervene." The IMF estimated total financial loss at 945 billion dollars, which aroused criticism from those who taxed it with being pessimistic. However, we'd still seen nothing yet.

In May, the Fed allocated 150 billion of guarantees to credit organizations, and 100 billion to deposit banks. At the same time, the government borrowed 165 billion dollars to reduce consumer tax.

Then came the worst: On June 30, 2008, the biggest insurance company in the world, AIG, announced that its financial division (which works like an investment bank in numerous swaps and hedges, in return for insuring the assets used to build up provisions), had issued CDSs linked to CDOs worth 441 billion dollars. Yet these CDOs, albeit graded AAA, were mostly founded on RMBS, some of which were subprimes, for 60 billion dollars. In other words, AIG admitted having counted in its technical reserve very speculative assets, securitized subprimes, of which the value was guaranteed by even more speculative mechanisms – a genuine time bomb!

However, one week later, the G8 summit was held in Tokayo, on the island of Hokkaido in Japan, from 7 – 9, July. The only subjects tackled were global warming, the food crisis, and the extension of the G8 to G13…

On July 15, the recession hit in with the price of oil falling by 17 dollars a barrel.

During this time, the securitization of subprimes was still making news: in July, the two public mortgage institutions, Freddie Mac and Fannie Mae, threatened not to repay their debt, estimated at 1.5T. Given that numerous financial institutions, particularly from Asia, had invested assets in these two infallible firms, the American finance minister, Mr. Paulson, announced, heartbroken, his intention to grant budgetary aid to Fannie Mae and Freddie Mac. All of his principles went against what he was obliged to say and do.

In August, consumer credit, in particular car loans went down. The ECB, just like the American Federal Bank boarded all possible securities without pre-checking, in order to support the banks.

On September 6, Lehman Brothers Bank, in turn, needed a 200 billion increase in capital: it admitted having 613 billion in debts and owning, amongst its assets, at least 85 billion worth of "toxic" securities, of which 57 billion derived from subprimes. As there was no income from these securities, the bank endured a considerable loss: 18 billion dollars during the last three quarters.

At the Ministry of Finance, nobody wanted to pay for Lehman Brothers, nor for AIG, nor for Morgan Stanley (also in a very ill state of health), nor for anyone else. Paulson thought that it was time to show that the federal budget was not there to pay for the turpitude of Wall Street! Everyone could see the danger of Lehman Brothers going bankrupt: the assets would have to be liquidized, of which CDOs and CDSs, which would lower their value and, according to the new IFRS standards, would oblige all other financial institutions to re-evaluate their own assets immediately at the same level. This would reduce their stock market value, and in accordance with the Basel accords, it would also reduce their loan capacity. Confronted with this threat, the Fed and the Treasury were convinced that the banks would bail Lehman Brothers out. There ensued a game of poker between Wall Street and Washington. The next day,

September 7, the Treasury was obliged to place Freddie Mac and Fannie Mae under conservatorship.

Paulson thought he was winning, during the weekend of Friday September 12 to Sunday 14, the Wall Street banks discussed a plan to confine Lehman's "bad" debts in a "bad bank" through 70 billion dollars in funding set up by other banks. The rest would be put into a "good bank" bought out by Barclay and the Bank of America. Everyone believed that the solution had been found. On Friday morning, the editor of the Financial Times wrote: "It is time for the authorities to step down (…). What has been done up until now should be enough."

Finally, on Monday morning, the Wall Street banks, convinced that Paulson would pay, rejected the plan as being too complicated to implement: what was a "bad bank?" The minister did not give in, and enraged, refused to step in. The same day, September 15, Lehman was placed under the protection of Chapter 11 of the law against bankruptcy. It was the worst decision that could have been made; in just a few days the whole of the world financial system was to be dragged to the edge of the abyss.

Even though the Fed was worried about the derivatives market becoming more problematic, it was actually the short term financial market that triggered the panic. Banks, not knowing exactly how much Lehman owed them, nor how much would be paid back, stopped lending money to anyone. The money market was completely paralyzed. The interbank market disappeared. LIBOR, the main stock market interest rate, crashed down by a few hundred base points (1 base point = 0.01%). As well as that, the same day, September 15, Lehman's bankruptcy forced AIG, already in great difficulty, to step in to play the role of the insurer which only increased its accumulated loss to 30 billion dollars, to which 600 million, linked to the devaluation of Fannie-Freddie shares after their nationalizations, can be added. That particular week, there was not one syndicated loan: long-term company financing stopped.

Rating agencies, obsessed with the necessity to make right past mistakes, immediately insisted that AIG give provisions, margin calls, of 13 billion, to compensate for the deterioration of its quality as insurer. AIG once again found itself in a liquidity crisis the security lost 95% of its value (1.25 dollars per share).

The next day, September 16, Paulson, as if he had understood the Lehman mistake could not be repeated, and terribly short of advisors, (apart from Goldman Sachs) still presumed that he could ask Goldman Sachs and J.P. Morgan to take charge of a consortium to organize a 75 billion syndicated loan for the insurer AIG. His efforts were in vain. From then on, the choice was between another bankruptcy and nationalization. Paulson could not inflict the same on AIG as he had on Lehman. For the first time, the Fed lent to a non-bank: 85 billion dollars guaranteed by all AIG assets at a penalizing rate so as to get repayment as soon as possible. However, that was the big change; once the loan was reimbursed, the Federal state would continue to be a 79.9% shareholder. To the amazement of everyone, the biggest insurance company in the world, the flagship of America, had been nationalized. Paulson also reserved the right to change the management, which he set to work at immediately, furious. As well as that, the next day, he was obliged to help out Goldman Sachs and Morgan Stanley, to prevent them being bought out by the Japanese or the English!

At this time in London, the situation was just as serious, but the crisis management was very different. All the experts dispersed throughout the City were asked to come to the Treasury. All started working on a plan, with the goal to save the City and its extraordinary financial privileges. The plan took the American mistakes into account; there was no question of letting the banks come close to bankruptcy, as had already happened once with Northern Rock. There was no question either of confining bad debts, as had been envisaged for Lehman. There was no question of the State providing financial resources without checking that they would really be used to finance businesses. Finally, there was no question of having a share in company profits without sitting on the board.

On September 25, the German finance minister, Peter Steinbruck, triumphantly declared that it was the end of

American as a superpower. Ten days later, he had to improvise a plan to save Hypo Real Estate from bankruptcy.

The month of September changed everything: Lehman went bankrupt, Bear Stearns and Merrill Lynch were bought out in a panic, Goldman Sachs and Morgan Stanley had been bailed out *in extremis*, and AIG had been nationalized. Once again, everyone thought that the crisis was over: the American government financed everything by increasing its debt that the credit rating agencies still thought worth the grade AAA, which is generally given to the safest borrowers. Nobody could see that on the CDSs market, that is to say the market of insurance against non-repayment of a loan, the probability of the United States defaulting, whilst still low, had doubled in six months: once again, CDSs had shown that the crisis was only just beginning.

CHAPTER 3

THE DAY CAPITALISM ALMOST DISAPPEARED

Towards the end of September 2008, nothing had been solved, in fact it was quite the contrary. Everyone understood that despite all the effort that had been made, confidence was still lacking. It was not enough that the Fed was supporting each bank, nor that another had gone bankrupt, nor did the tax incentives granted to subprime holders help. This was the case in the United States and elsewhere.

Everywhere, bank clients were asking themselves questions and everywhere, lenders were taking their savings out of the more speculative funds. Others were even wondering if their money was really safe in the banks. American businesses were finding it more and more difficult to obtain credit from banks, and their treasury, in the form of shares, had lost a lot of its value. The American economy was close to suffocating, and the rest of the world with it. On September 26, under pressure from the banks, and in spite of an absolutely opposing ideology, the Bush administration finally stepped in. The Treasury secretary, Paulson, offered to buy the banks' bad debts at a "fair price" and he reserved the right to fix it irrevocably. Therefore, it was a confinement plan, just like the one that had been envisaged and refused for Lehman just a few weeks earlier.

Criticism rang out from all over the country, the Congress and the Senate. The left wing asked: How can "good" and "bad" debts be distinguished? What is a "fair" price? Won't Paulson favor his old friends from Goldman Sachs, or even all the Wall Street banks? Would it not be better to nationalize these banks? Or at least to impose rigorous rules? Why force the country into more debt when in the long term that means increasing taxes? Is that not risking a fatal hit to the dollar and ruining all Americans financially? Why not use the available money, if it really exists, to support the poorest households that are at risk of losing their homes? Why not even cancel the debts of these households just as the Roosevelt administration did in its time?

Criticism also came from the right wing: Why is the state interfering in private sector business? Why finance "casino capitalism?" Why encourage banks to commit mistakes by subsidizing them? Why not let the banks solve their own problems? Why increase public debt, recruit civil servants, and increase tax? Why should the taxpayer pay the bonuses of bankers, ex-post, who got us into this situation in the first place?

The Republican Representatives and Senators opposed to the Paulson plan, suggested creating a mutual guarantee fund for banks financed by the banks themselves, instead of public support.

On September 29, despite all the effort made by the Bush administration, the House of Representatives rejected the Paulson plan by 228 votes to 205. The bank system was battered. Panic was at its highest point. Wall Street fell by 777 points.

That day, we came close to the breakdown of the world financial system. The liquidity crisis immediately spread to Europe and Asia, provoking sudden increases in one and three month rates in Singapore, Hong Kong and Sydney. The Bank of Japan also increased the rates and the cost of its interventions.

In the night from Monday 29, to Tuesday 30, September, European banks borrowed 15.5 billion euros from the European Central Bank.

On Tuesday 30, September, the crisis intensified. The banks were preciously keeping their own liquidities, creating a shortage of money. The hedge funds anticipated the fall of the banks by forward selling their assets, speculating on their decrease and provoking it to the displeasure of the bankers. Even the most credit-worthy businesses had difficulty obtaining short-term loans. Europe was also affected. All its banks were threatened. To get through, the central banks injected considerable quantities of liquidities. The Fed, that had never had to control an investment bank, now also covered the losses through no-questions-asked loans: the special rediscount limit went from 300 to 450 billion dollars. The ECB and the Bank of Japan's commitments doubled. In the same day, the Australian Central Bank injected 1.6 billion U.S. dollars into its banks by taking securities in trust, as all the other central banks were doing. Despite that, short-term rates leapt up to 10% in London and the volume of transactions crashed.

The same day, September 30, Fitch, wanting to rid itself of past mistakes by showing newfound severity, marked down the grade given to the American insurer Hartford Financial, a victim of consecutive losses due to Lehman's bankruptcy and the state buy-out of AIG. This new grade provoked an 18% decrease in the stock market value of shares in this company and the next day, the decrease in the stock market value of two other insurers, Metropolitan Life and Genworth Financial.

Everybody realized it was time to react. The American state had to be authorized to finance losses in order to reestablish confidence. The Paulson plan was re-written hastily following the model that Gordon Brown was about to announce in London, which envisaged 500 billion pounds to help numerous banks: there was no more question of confining "bad" debts!

Paulson suggested to Congress that the Treasury granted a 700 billion dollar guarantee to the banks and other financial institutions, of which 250 billion on mortgages, a 1,500 billion guarantee on bank debts, and another 500 billion on savings accounts. To try to convince the stubborn Congress members, he conceded that the Treasury would ask for Congress authorization for certain measures. Nothing was planned to help out the hedge funds.

To put these measures into practice, Paulson suggested creating the Trouble Asset Relief Program (TARP) which would be managed by the Office of Financial Stability and would organize the buying out of all mortgage-backed securities, mortgage loans from regional banks and bad quality asset insurance. Once again the idea of a "bad bank" came back through grouping and confining the bad loans. The TARP would finance the recapitalization of banks and companies in need of capital; it would give assistance to indebted households.

The Paulson plan came with some condition precedents: the directors' salaries would be limited, the government agencies would sit on the board of the bailed out businesses and the funds lent would be reimbursed with future income.

The Senate was hesitant. Many were sincerely shocked by what they likened to socialism. Others cynically bargained away their votes: this way allowing for the extension of a tax on rum from Puerto Rico and the Virgin Islands, the possibility of letting racing circuits spread their losses over seven years, and the transfer of certain taxes on the importation of wool products to a wool fund were decided....

On Friday October 3, the Senate voted in favor of the plan (74 votes for, 25 against). The House of Representatives still needed to give their consent. It lingered on. During the weekend, the situation got worse. Many very big businesses were about to go bankrupt through lack of working capital. It was also the case for certain states, including California which needed 7 billion dollars in order to meet emergency payments. For the first time since the beginning of the financial crisis in August 2007, nothing was under control; the 1929 spectrum seemed to be coming back.

On Saturday October 4, there was a meeting in Paris between the leaders of France, Germany, Italy and Great Britain, called on the initiative of the temporary president of the European Union, the French President. The meeting only resulted in a vague agreement of a guarantee given to banks and the lifting of the restraints concerning budget deficits. No European funding was set up. The banks were to be rescued state by state. Even though during the night the German Chancellor, (who had refused to group together the risks so as not to pay for others) found out that it was her own banks which were going to suffer the most! In fact, the crisis of the

Hypo Real Estate bank obliged the German government to pay out more than 50 billion euros...

The European financial traders viewed the results of this conference as disastrous. The rates increased. (LIBOR for loans in pounds, Euribor for three month loans in euros). Some banks were prepared to pay 11% interest, five times more than in June! Only the Treasury Departments and the central banks continued to feed the monetary market. The self-control of the ECB governor and the French president of the European Union were to play a major role in this particular phase of the crisis.

On Monday October 6, confronted with worldwide panic, the House of Representatives approved the Paulson plan by a large majority (263 votes against 171) without managing to reestablish confidence. It was too little too late, as many people thought! The FDIC (Federal Deposit Insurance Corp., a federal agency for bank deposit guarantees), which receives an almost unlimited line of credit from the Treasury in order to help banks threatened with bankruptcy, declared it did not have the human means necessary to check whether the funds allocated to these banks were being used correctly.

The amounts mentioned in the Paulson plan started to be released: 250 billion dollars were used to force holdings in nine main American banks. 123 billion dollars were used to bail out AIG, probably to buy back CDSs that came from Lehman. Interbank loan transactions did not take off again.

On October 7, the IMF estimated the planetary loss at 1.4T against 0.9T in March. The next day, all European banks were threatened. Several were nationalized during the day: Great Britain took over the Bradford & Bingley, 75% of the Belgian part of Fortis (which was very much affected by the American crisis) were taken over by BNP Paribas with holdings taken by the Belgian and Luxembourg governments and Ireland guaranteed 400 billion euros of debts and deposits.

On October 8, Gordon Brown announced the plan he had been working on for three weeks: the state taking a massive stake in the capital of British banks, accompanied by debt guarantees and strict control of the use of funds.

On Thursday October 9, the American government granted a further 37.8 billion dollar loan to AIG, whose deficit was seemingly a bottomless pit.

That same day, Nouriel Roubini repeated that the bankruptcy of the world financial system was close. Many countries, of which Iceland and Hungary, indebted by heavy external deficit, saw their hedge funds pull out their capital, and their stock markets crash. Italy had to pay a 1% higher interest rate than Germany to raise money, when this difference had been three times less just six months before. In China, the real estate market showed signs of cracking and factory closures multiplied with businesses finding themselves deprived of their outlets in western countries.

In the United States, the main monolines (of which Ambac and MBIA), in which nobody any longer had confidence, announced disastrous results: their losses had been multiplied by nearly seven in one year, and a significant part of the remaining 450 billion dollars of the Paulson plan would have to go towards rescuing them and consumer credit agencies such as GE Financial Services.

On Saturday October 11, the four institutional leaders of the European Union (the presidents of the Council, the Commission, the Central Bank and the Eurogroup), met, unlike the previous Saturday when it was four member states that met, for a meeting in Paris initiated once again by France and President Sarkozy, and decided to coordinate an intervention following the British model: a state guarantee would be given for all new debt until the end of 2009, taking a stake in the banks' capital, and if necessary, a return to the old accounting system which allowed the value of assets to be maintained on a permanent basis and so the lending capacity of the banks as well. In total, Europe guaranteed 1,700 billion euros, of which 840 were for the Franco-German team. The majority of these 1,700 billion concerned guarantees and bank recapitalization for 250 billion. On October 13, France committed to an amount of 360 billion, of which 40 would be used to recapitalize banks and 320 for bank guarantees. However, it was not a triumph: there was no real joint action and no action came from the commission or from the ECB. There was no specific European budget.

On the 18, in Washington, presidents Bush, Sarkozy and Barroso showed willing to recapitalize the banks and financial institutions, and allocate them an unlimited provision of liquidities, give temporary guarantees on all deposits, grant businesses credit through buying trade paper, buy out all "toxic" real estate products (in the United States) according to clear criteria and open valorizations, to use the IMF and all regional development banks to grant credit to developing countries, and to implement a laxer monetary political theory. Finally, if necessary, they agreed to organize a series of international G20 summits as an informal forum grouping together the countries that represent 90% of the world GDP for better regulations, better supervision and control of rating agencies, hedge funds, earnings and tax havens. We can measure the incredible change these people have gone through; just a month earlier they nearly all thought that the best thing to do was nothing, that deregulation and free market trade was the key to economic and political success. However, the change was only minor: in 2009, Great Britain is to preside over the G20, and it is not in her best interest to reform money markets. The first of these summits was planned for November 15, 2008, in Washington.

On October 21, all were worried about the settlement of the part of the Lehman bankruptcy concerning the

CDSs, which was to be sorted out the same day. The initial value seemed to have been 400 billion dollars and their crash risked taking the statements of account of other banks with them. In fact, nothing happened because these CDSs had been absorbed for the most part by loans from the Fed and AIG, a counterpart most exposed to the Lehman Brothers bankruptcy. The other linked CDSs remained, for the time being, hidden in the balance sheets...

On October 22, the futures market was suspended. On the 23, Roubini once again predicted the possible closure of the stock markets. AIG announced that it needed more than the 122.8 billion dollars already borrowed from the state. On Friday October 24, the 79th anniversary of the fall of Wall Street, was another black day: the Dow Jones index went down 3.59%. In Paris the CAC 40 index dropped by 3.54%, after having gone under the 3,000 point mark. Tokyo lost 9.60% and Bombay 11%.

In London, everyone realized that the City was much oversized, and the financial production exaggerated, soon there would be a need for fewer banks. Almost overnight, these overpaid people who had been made redundant were viewed as outcasts by their colleagues.

On October 26, Iceland, which was on the verge of bankruptcy, given that its three main banks, which were very dependent on hedge funds, were ruined, signed an agreement with the International Monetary Fund for a 2.1 billion dollar loan (1.7 billion euros). The list of other countries in great difficulty continued to grow: Ukraine, Pakistan, Argentina, Hungary, etc.

On October 27, the demand for liquidities was still very high; hoarding led to an exponential demand by businesses looking for working capital. The Fed became the last resort buyer of unsecuritized debt for an amount that could attain 1.6T.

On October 30, AIG had to put in a claim for more funds from the Treasury once again. It was then established that there were at least 400 billion worth of CDSs in AIG; the insurer had been using pseudo-insurance! The AIG aid plan went from 123 to 150 billion dollars in the form of longer-term loans than originally planned: securities, CDSs and MBAS were placed in a new "vehicle."

Once again many estimated that the worst of the crisis was over: the stock market indexes started to go up, like the CAC 40 that went from 3000 on October 27 to 3700 on November 4. The monetary market rates slowly came back to an almost normal level. Oil continued to decrease (from 73 dollars the barrel on October 21, to 61 dollars on November 10.)

However, this was just a brief respite; nothing had been solved and the "toxic" products were still there, on the bank balance sheets. Consumption was crumbling away. Debt reduction continued. Assets lost their value. It was the automobile industry that was now on the brink of bankruptcy, in the United States as well as in Europe.

On November 9, (one week after the election of Barrack Obama as president of the United States) the G20 finance ministers met to prepare for the next summit. China was worried about the social consequences of a drop of more than 9% in the rate of economic growth (which would make very difficult the creation of 30 million jobs that are necessary every year because of mere rural migration); a 586 billion dollar (4 trillion yen, or 15% of China's GDP) stimulus plan was launched to invest between now and the end of 2010 in infrastructures to buy wheat for country people and to support small and middle-sized businesses, in particular in rural areas, with tax allowances for the middle class. China could easily do much more: there is still a surplus of its global budget, even though state expenditure goes up by 30% per year.

On November 10, the finance ministers from the Union agreed to suggest a reform founded on five principles: to supervise credit rating agencies, particularly because of their impact on the capital requirements imposed by the Basel-II Accords, to harmonize the accounting rules, to control the financial market players' earnings, to forbid offshore markets, to give the IMF the main responsibility and necessary resources to reestablish confidence.

The same day in the United States, the situation continued to deteriorate: it was announced that 240,000 jobs had been lost in October, the same amount as in

September. AIG still appeared to be a bottomless pit and announced a new loss of 24.5 billion for the third quarter, when the American authorities had already granted more than 150 billion dollars. The same day, Fannie Mae also announced a new loss of over 29 billion dollars for the third quarter 2008 only.

On November 12, Mr. Paulson denounced the Europeans and the Chinese as being responsible for the crisis and renounced on buying out the "bad" assets from banks! He modified his plan to be able to invest directly in the banks.

On November 14, the European Commission announced its intention of protesting at the WTO against the budgetary aid that the United States provided for its automobile industry, and to organize the coordination of the national revival plan for the twenty-seven member states.

The G20 summit held on November 15, did not reach any conclusion, except to put off the reforms until a later G20 summit to be held in April in London, under British presidency. Therefore things were still deadlocked: the financial system remained paralyzed and the economic recession began. Everyone set up plans of national reforms, but no comprehensive reform, particularly for regulation. Only the central banks continued to finance the banks (and even some businesses in the United States). Everything pointed towards the risk of a depression for 2009.

Following some tragedies in the City of London, the big banks decided, without so much as mentioning it openly, that they would no longer make redundancies on Fridays because of the number of suicides during the weekends that immediately follow redundancy announcements.

*

*　　*

On November 18, the Belgian legal system authorized the handover of the majority of Fortis to BNP Paribas. On November 20, for the first time since May 2003, the CAC 40 closed below the 3,000 point mark, whilst Wall Street closed at its lowest for more than five years. The stock market value of oil fell under 50 dollars a barrel in New York. On November 21, Dominique Strauss-Kahn advised: "not to lock ourselves up in straitjackets" For the managing director of the IMF, the 3% public deficit limit imposed by the European stability pact did not have to be respected to "the closest decimal point." Argentina nationalized its pension funds, teetering on the brink of bankruptcy.

On November 24, Great Britain unveiled a 20 billion pound revival plan, in other words almost 1% of the United Kingdom's GDP. The United States president-elect, Barack Obama, called for an "immediate" economic stimulus plan to break away from the "vicious circle" of crisis.

On November 26, the European Commission presented the total amount of the European stimulus plans: 200 billion euros. On November 28, we learnt that the unemployment rate in the euro zone attained 7.7% in October. The British government, which had guaranteed an increase in capital for the Royal Bank of Scotland, became the majority shareholder with 57.9% of the shares.

On December 1, José Manuel Barroso called for a "very clear" drop in the ECB's interest rates. On December 4, the Crédit Suisse announced a 1.95 billion euro loss and envisaged 5,300 job cuts (11% of its workforce.) The European Central Bank dropped its main intervention rate by 0.75 points to 2.50%, the strongest reduction in its history, preparing for a recession in the euro zone in 2009. The Bank of England dropped its intervention rate by one point, bringing it to 2%, to the level of the 1940s.

On December 11, the announcement came that unemployment in the United States had attained its highest level since 1982, affecting 4.4 million Americans. On December 12, the United States Senate rejected the automobile industry rescue plan. Bernard Madoff, ex-president of NASDAQ was arrested, accused of the fraud of nearly 50 billion dollars. General Motors admitted preparing to file for bankruptcy. It looked as if there was no interrupting the disaster.

On December 13, two banks went bankrupt in the United States. On December 15, some French banks announced that they had been affected by Madoff's fraud. On December 17, the Fed reduced its main interest rate to a range between zero and 0.25%, the lowest level ever recorded.

On December 20, George Bush, unruffled, considered that the 17.4 billion dollars (12.4 billion euros) of the emergency federal automobile plan should help the American manufacturers to come out of the crisis "reinforced."

On December 30, in Tokyo, the Nikkei index finished the year 2008 on its worst annual percentage fall of its history: -42.12%. The Frankfort stock market lost 40.4% in one year. The Shanghai stock market finished 2008 with a loss of 65%. The CAC 40 lost 42.68% of its value in 2008 and the London stock market lost 31.33%.

On January 2, 2009, the Bank of England dropped its intervention rate to 1.5%, the lowest in the history of the bank, founded in 1694. Barack Obama presented his 775 billion dollar stimulus plan.

On January 12, the German coalition adopted a 50 billion euro stimulus plan, after having postponed it for a long time. George W. Bush asked the Congress, in the name of his successor, Barack Obama, to release the second half of the Paulson funds of 700 billion dollars.

All the banks announced disastrous fourth quarters. On January 16, Citigroup announced a loss of 19 billion dollars and split into two entities. On January 20, the Royal bank of Scotland announced a 28 billion pound loss for 2008, its stock market value had lost more than 70% since the beginning of 2009. The Bank of England allowed businesses to borrow directly over the counter. On January 22, the pound sterling attained its lowest level ever compared to the dollar for nearly 24 years. **The same day, Microsoft, the emblematic company representing the American knowledge-based economy, announced more than 5,000 lay-offs for 2009. Silicon Valley had been caught by the crisis. Timothy Geithner, the Secretary of the Treasury, then declared that China had "manipulated" its currency in order to support exports, and pleaded for a return of the "strong dollar."** The same day, Microsoft, the emblematic company representing the American knowledge-based economy, announced more than 5,000 lay-offs for 2009. Silicon Valley had been caught by the crisis. Timothy Geithner, the Secretary of the Treasury, then declared that China had "manipulated" its currency in order to support exports, and pleaded for a return of the "strong dollar."

It was becoming clearer and clearer that it was going to be necessary to isolate the toxic products (but how? How much? Where? At what price?). Speculation was also going to have to be controlled, particularly against the bank shares.

On January 23, the CAC 40 closed at 2781 points, even lower than on November 21, 2008, the same level as in April 2003. Bank shares continued to cause concern: between the 19, and 23, January, BNP shares lost 28% of their value.

Just in the day of January 26, 70,000 people were made redundant in Europe and in the United States.

February 9, the French state lent 6 billion euros to French automobile manufacturers to support the industry. Renault and Peugeot agreed not to resort to layoff plans in France. On February 10, the "Geithner Plan" was presented. This 787 billion dollar stimulus plan, described as complex, aims to get credit flowing again (notably through "joint" securitization – public-private – of CDOs), to rescue American real estate, to help small companies, to strengthen the balance sheet of banks and notably their capital. On February 13, it was announced that France's 2008 deficit had jumped to 56 billion euros due to an 11 billion euro decrease in government revenues (corporate tax collection) whereas spending had risen by more than 7 billion. The euro zone GDP had fallen by 1.5% in the forth quarter of 2008. On February 22, the need for tougher supervision of financial markets and hedge funds was the subject of

a consensus of European leaders brought together in Berlin to prepare for the G20.

On February 27, the unemployment rate in the euro zone had reached 8.2%, with more than 13 million unemployed. Italy, Spain and Ireland were particularly affected. The Royal Bank of Scotland lost 27 billion pounds, the greatest loss ever recorded by a company in the United Kingdom. American GDP fell by 6.2% in the forth quarter of 2008, much more than had been predicted.

On March 3, the Tokyo Stock Exchange closed at its lowest level in twenty-six years. It was the beginning of a bullish rally on the main international financial centers, allowing them to recover around 20% in six weeks. On March 10, Dominique Strauss-Kahn declared that "the IMF expects global economic growth to slow down to be below zero this year, its worst performance" since World War II. March 14, Alistair Darling, the British Chancellor of the Exchequer, announced that the G20 would take "all the necessary measures" to protect large financial institutions, to stabilize to world financial system and to stimulate credit.

On March 15, the news came out that the American Insurer AIG was planning to pay out almost 450 million dollars in bonuses to its executives in 2009. On March 22, The United States expected a budgetary deficit of 1,800 billion dollars for 2009, the equivalent of the GDP of France or the United Kingdom.

April 2, the London G20 Summit reached a consensus on the necessity of all countries to massively intervene in order to restore confidence in the markets and to save the global economy from bankruptcy. The IMF's role was strengthened. Almost 1T was to be injected into the world economy through various means. No decisions were made regarding Anglo-Saxon tax havens, or on increasing the capital of banks. The same day, the accounting rules of Anglo-Saxon banks were changed, no longer allowing them to re-evaluate their assets on the value of the market, thus greatly improving the value of their capital.

Since then, some action has been taken: the efforts of the French president to push for a serious review of regulation; the promised list of tax havens, the improved supervision of rating agencies, hedge funds and the salaries of company directors and traders, the creation of a Financial Stability Board (instead of the Forum of the same name); the efforts of the American president to evoke the great stimulus programs; the efforts of the Chinese president to reform the IMF and to create SDRs; those of southern hemisphere presidents to increase the funds of the IMF by 0.75 trillion in their favour; the raising of 5 trillion in stimulus funds. All of these measures and these declarations cannot diminish the fear that many other clouds may appear on the horizon, because in attempting to resolve this crisis we are using the same weapons which created it. Here are a few examples:

Five Trillion for stimulus plans? This is the amount that has already been freed up; a mix of loans and money issuing, which represents 10% of world GDP, but which brings up the simple question: who is financing this? I have not seen any revenue, except for the sale of some IMF gold; and even then, putting this on the market will bring its price down. How can we hope to resolve a debt crisis by increasing debt? Over time, it will be with taxpayers' money.

Healthier bank balance sheets? By allowing banks and insurers to no longer re-evaluate their assets at prices close to their market value, we can improve the appearance of bank balance sheets. However, we are not encouraging them to get rid of their toxic assets. With these new measures, auditors will even find themselves obliged to validate the valuation of assets even when they are not convinced by their underlying assumptions. When the truth surfaces, in a few months or a few years, these institutions will need to be recapitalized... with taxpayers' money (*again*)!

Reduced speculation? In appearance, yes – but in practice? Nothing has been said about CDSs, the sword of Damocles hanging over the system, or about Anglo-Saxon tax havens, the big winners of the G20, or about the reality of securitization and leverage. In fact, everything seems to be carrying on just like before: the FSA (the English regulator) has allowed Barclays to sell one of its subsidiaries by allowing it to finance the buyer – just like before. The new authorized valuations will artificially improve capital and allow leverage to rise. Just like before! The Geithner plan will allow American banks to sell their toxic assets with leverage worthy of the worst speculations from before the crisis (9:1). How can the Financial Stability Board allow practices that are so contrary to the principles it is supposed to be defending? How can it allow speculative funds to make such immense profits with taxpayers' money (*once again*)?

Finally, as nothing has really been done to strengthen the capital of banks, on which the sustainable regeneration of healthy financing of demand depends, the G20 seems to be waiting for the bankruptcy of many financial institutions, and to be trying to protect itself from its own failure, by this reassuring and terrifying sentence: "We will put in place credible strategies from the measures that need to be taken…" In other words, if everything we are doing does not work, we will do even more! But more of what? More debt. And, eventually, more taxes (*yet again*)!

In all, the actions are unfortunately being carried out as if, alongside very useful and brave measures, we are putting in place a large-scale, but blind, stimulus plan, not directed towards saving the banks nor towards future industries, and not financed, which could end in bankruptcies, hyperinflation and a formidably severe plan in two months or in two years.

All of this is being conducted as if led by a group from Alcoholics Anonymous, all happy with their good resolutions, decided upon leaving their meeting to go out for one last drink... for the road.

On April 9, the Sumitomo bank, one of the three largest Japanese banks, announced a loss of almost 4 billion dollars over the last twelve months.

A slight improvement was seen on April 12, the first quarter results of American banks were better than expected, some had even made a profit, such as Citi, coming out of the red for the first time since the third quarter of 2007.

April 15, the number one Swiss bank, UBS, announced a loss of 1.3 billion euros for the first quarter, and 8,700 layoffs by the end of 2010.

On April 18, the president of the ECB, Jean-Claude Trichet, ruled out the possibility of cutting the benchmark rate to close to zero by indicating that this would not be "appropriate" for the European Economic situation.

April 24, the G20 Finance Ministers met in Washington to check the progress of the measures agreed at the G20 in London.

For some, a miracle for getting out of the crisis is in the works: with the combination of the Geithner plan (which allows investment funds and banks to buy the toxic assets of other banks by borrowing mainly from the American federal budget) and accounting changes (which allow banks to re-evaluate these assets at a higher price), we can see a derivatives market settling in where very expensive assets are sold to some, only to buy others for an even higher price. This is how an asset-price "bubble" will form entirely funded by taxes. The valuation of the capital of banks, so far totally corrupted by the presence of toxic products, will naturally be raised without the state paying over more money other than that which would allow banks to buy these products and to increase their price. Growth could thus take off, creating new financial fortunes in the midst of countless industrials bankruptcies.

This bubble is already forming. We can measure it by the divergence between the share market in full growth (in particular those of risk sectors, financial ones more than others) and that of the totally anaemic credit market; as well as by the difference between the negative evolution of forecasted profit and the positive evolution of shares, or even with the increase of using multiples for the valuation of companies, or the foreseeable nature of the shares of central banks, which allows the return of exchange transfer mechanisms, carry trade, on the dollar and the yen. Soon, this bubble alone could give us the impression that the crisis is over: banks will be creditworthy once again, they will pay back what they have borrowed from the state, and thus earn back the right to pay out bonuses; the increase in financial assets will stimulate investment, employment and growth. The unemployed and taxpayers will have reactivated the bonus pump that employees and lenders can no longer feed.

An optimistic outlook before the crisis takes off with the above – but it has already. We could even say that those who had predicted the worst crisis since 1929 wanted to make themselves seem interesting, that capitalism was still resilient and that the American economy did not need global regulation to try to curb its dynamism.

We could hope that this scenario will happen: an immoral exit to the crisis is better than depression. But, unfortunately, nothing would be resolved: the risks would still be there, for the survival of companies, retirement, the value of assets, jobs or the management of public debt. We could thus ask ourselves how a democratic president could work for the benefit of such a scandalous manoeuvre so that a few bankers are able to rebuild their fortunes with taxpayers' money, the latter having no power over the banks. Faced with these persistent risks, consumers will start living in quite a different way, that is to say, by saving, buying during sale periods, turning away from pretension and changing their lifestyle. Companies just like countries will have to create a new balance. The G20 can thus no longer avoid the reforms it carefully evaded in London.

In the meantime, if Europe manages to withstand the illusion of the Geithner bubble, it will have a unique opportunity to pull a little ahead of the United States by mastering its own financial system, which would be in everyone's interest. To do so, it must have the courage to reform, even when everyone wants to believe that the crisis is over...

*

*   *

It is time to evaluate the situation for the first time. Out of an estimated total of 4.1T of world bank shareholders' equitycapital, for the moment the losses reach 2.2T according to the IMF and 3.6T according to Roubini for the United States alone, to which 4.5T of doubtful consumer credit (just in the United States) can be added; Standard & Poor's estimated that it could cost taxpayers up to a total of 10 GNP points (1T). Roubini estimated at around 3T. Today, only 0.8T of losses have been financed. The total loss on loans is 3.6T, of which 1.8 in the United States. The total world bank loans (84T) equals 18 times the amount of shareholders' equitycapital of these financial institutions' capital instead of the 15 authorized. Even for some of the most respectable banks, this ratio is 50! An injection of shareholders' equity of 1.73T in capital is necessary for the global American banking system not to go bankrupt. The drop in the share market and real estate has provoked the destruction of about 60T of nominal wealth. World economic growth for 2009 will be negativeis predicted, at the best, to be nil, with a depression of at least 5% in the United States and 42% in Europe.

When President Obama came into power, he wais confronted with gigantic financial stakes: a budgetary deficit of 12%, or 1.3T, a total United States debt of 54T, the banking system bankrupt and industry about to crash. Unless we can believe that the reestablishment will take place solely through the markets and the bubble created only by le jeu du marché and the bubble will allow to create for a while the Geithner plan, new resources are necessary. Where are they going to come from?

Where could the necessary money come from to reestablish confidence? From the American taxpayers' pocket, which would destroy any hope of economic growth returning? From the deficit, which would soon render American treasury bonds and the dollar disreputable?

CHAPTER 4

THREATS STILL TO COME

Considered from the point of view of all employees', the economic situation is not, for now, much more difficult at in the beginningmiddle of 2009 than it was a year earlier. Unemployment has not gone up a lot yet. The drop in real estate allows more people the hope of buying a home, if they obtain a loan. The erosion of economic growth has massively reduced the price of oil and encouraged competition between producers and distributors. From a shareholder's point of view, the decrease in stock markets has brought the value of their portfolios back to what it was five years ago, when the holders had no reason to complain. In addition, most think that the worst is over, that the enormous resources deployed, combined with today's significant technological and demographic strength, and the drop in price of raw materials will make it possible to smooth over the cracks, stabilize banks and quickly return to strong economic growth and full employment.

However, it is nothing of the sort. Even if the current financial crisis were quickly curbed which is unlikely to be the case, the economic crisis itself is only just beginning. If no major planetary plan is put in place quickly, the crisis will profoundly affect the majority of businesses, consumers, workers, savers, borrowers and nations for a long time. In some countries, it may even degenerate into a social and political crisis. All the ideology of our worry-free societies will be questioned; we will probably look for scapegoats rather than the causes and solutions. Democracy itself risks being threatened.

The real nature of what is coming is as yet uncertain: will this be a crisis like 1929, where the world quickly went from abysmal deflation of financial assets to a profound economic depression which was only ended by a war? Or will it be a long and troubled period towards the unknown, like the stretch of time between 1971 and 1982 when the United States was in turmoil which finished on a high point thanks to revolutionary technical innovation, the microprocessor, with its three nomadic applications: the mobile phone, the laptop computer and the Internet?

With both hypotheses, it is likely that we will have to pass through a series of new disasters. The worst scenario is therefore easy to outline: the banks, worried about their own futures and in spite of public guarantees, will be more and more reluctant to lend to businesses, and thus a lot will go bankrupt. Other financial institutions (from hedge funds to credit card companies which are now weakened,) will crash, provoking a drop in the value of property. Many countries will find it difficult to finance these losses and to borrow on international markets. Countries with savings, like China, will lose parts of their reserves and will repatriate what is left to support their own, internal economic growth. Progressively, they will give up on the dollar whose stabilization will threaten European economies. Depression will bring a massive price drop that even ample revival through public spending will not be enough to slow down. Two to five years of depression will follow, the time necessary to erase the principal debts of western countries, probably through inflation caused by the immense monetary injections.

Is that excessive pessimism? I hope so! Unless this scenario has already begun.

The New Stakes of the Financial System

American and European banks, which are the object of all sorts of concern, and in the end, of controls, are far from being out of the woods. InAt the middleend of 20098, they had so far provisioned for only a quarter of known losses and a tenth of probable losses. Many of them, as we have seen, are technically bankrupt. There remain many unknown facts about how they rushed towards the illusion of derivative products that then became untraceable, and about the amounts that now must be considered as lost. For example, the withdrawal concerning the so-called Alt-A mortgage loans (not quite as bad as subprimes) will increase next year and continue increasing until 2011. Moreover, there are even more Alt-As (1T) than subprimes (0.9T) shared out between the numerous American banks, from Fannie Mae to Wachovia, which were all in a hurry to benefit from these miracle products. The case for securitized products in general is the same; many trillions no longer have any value. As the securitization market has dried up, banks will have to keep the majority of any new loans on their balance sheets, just at the same time as the risk is increasing. In particular the CDS market, which today represents successive transactions worth more than 60T, could collapse if nobody wanted to carry the risk. Five percent of bankruptcies on products insured by CDSs would create more than 3T worth of debt default. Consequently, banks will remain fragile for a long time, and will protect their own equity capital to the detriment of their loans.

In fact, according to the regulations imposed between central banks by the Basel-II Accords, Tier 1 (the money they have at their disposal and the business securities of which they own at least 20%) must represent at least 7%

of the amount of bank loans (in reality, it is more complicated). That is to say that banks must lend less than 15 times what they have in the safe. If they exceed this ratio (and they do, by a lot), they will need to find new funds or reduce their loans, which would deepen the recession.

Furthermore, the central banks, not wishing to be accused of being overly lax, will one day probably want to change this ratio from 7 to 9%, that is to say that banks will not be allowed to lend more than 12 times their resources. To satisfy the future regulators' requirements, the shareholders' equitycapital in all banks worldwide will have to be increased by 3T.

Today, only governments would be crazy enough to invest such amounts in banks. Therefore, they will have the choice between at least partial nationalization or a massive credit reduction.

Nationalization or depression? These are the choices. It has already been made for all governments, left or right. Nationalizations have, for that matter, already started in Great Britain and Ireland. They still have to find considerable sums.

The number of establishments will noticeably be reduced to only a few oligopolies in the main countries. The investment banks, which will no longer be able to make miraculous profits out of imaginary securitized products will be unable to remain independent and will merge with deposit banks. Bank profitability will be massively reduced: deposits, the cheapest banking resource, will become more and more sought after, and so more and more expensive. Even the international financial institutions (like the EIB, the European Investment Bank), will find it difficult to borrow below LIBOR.

All the non-banking financial actors will also be threatened with extinction: insurers, hedge funds, monetary funds, private equity firms which make unbelievable profits, credit card issuers, monolines, (real magic boxes without justification), brokers and mortgage lenders. All will suffer from the worsening of refinancing conditions because of their newly lowered grades given by credit raters compelled to be more severe in order to justify their own existence. All will try to sidle up to the bank counter thanks to the Paulson and Obama and European plans. Credit card issuers, like GE Capital will ask to become banks in order to benefit from the support of states. This will also be the case for credit subsidiaries of automobile producers and big box stores. Households will be made bankrupt; in the United States in particular, students will find themselves incapable of paying back their loans. In particular, hedge funds will be in real danger, as they are using money that will be sorely needed elsewhere. As they have often gambled in the opposite direction of monetary evolution and the rate of raw materials, they will be increasingly compelled to settle their positions and sell off their assets cheaply (for an amount around 10T), as they are now incapable of borrowing (because banks, having become increasingly cautious, bear a grudge against the hedge funds for having speculated for a fall in their securities in September and October 2008) or investing their securitized instruments. Those subscribers who still have payments due will terminate their contracts. At least half of these funds will disappear which could have even more disastrous consequences on the financial system than the Lehman Brother's bankruptcy and the bailing out of RBS. Therefore, it is probable that a huge debt reduction program will have to be set up for speculative funds, either by the private sector, which is almost financially impossible (nobody wants to help them), or by the central banks and national budgets (which would prove very difficult to do, politically speaking).

Finally, the ultimate financial threat: the complete freezing of the credit system by savers themselves if they forbid banks from investing their savings. For example, the Fed, which has 0.8T on its balance sheet to operate on a credit market worth more than 50T, could still create money; but that would be pointless if all bank account holders decided to keep only cash in their accounts and did not allow the banking system to use that money.

Threatened Insurers

In the most developed countries in the world where insecurity had become politically unbearable, everyone wanted to protect themselves against risks: citizens against illness and old age, companies against economic risks. Public and private security and protection systems were set up, especially in the form of insurance companies. To prove that they could actually cover the damages they claim to guarantee, these companies have, in principle, a buffer reserve, that they invest for the well-being of everyone. Just like banks, they have to respect certain rules, called Solvency I, which ensures that the insurers will have, at the given time, the means to cope with the risks that they cover and that they have an almost zero probability (0.5 %) of going bankrupt within a year.

In particular, they have to publish a "solvency margin" every six months, the proportion between the total of their life insurance policies (their debt towards savers) and the provisions constituted to manage their non-life insurance policies (their debt towards economic agents), and their capital.

The latter is the total of the insurance company's capital, its subordinate debt and an estimate of the profits the company could make available from its investments, which are thus not evaluated on their immediate market value, but according to a long term value generally calculated using mathematical models.

All of this gives very uncertain values: *firstly*, because it supposes that the law of large numbers is at play and that a buyer always finds a seller, which did not turn out to be true for banks. *Secondly*, because insurers, victims of overly low interest rates, in promising their clients overly high returns, invested a large share of their reserves in very risky products, in credit default swaps (CDSs), certain types of insurance policies, hidden in hedge funds or structured bonds, and even in derivative products of these same CDSs! *Finally*, because with the crisis, certain investments that were considered very safe, such as bonds from banking institutions, were depreciated by the risk of the latter being potentially nationalized at a paltry value.

Estimates

In all, the solvency ratios of insurers have become very fragile. As the insurance sector is not regulated on an international scale, the International Association of Insurance Supervisors (IAIS), which brings together all insurance regulators, does not even publish statistics. We only have estimates to go on: it seems that insurance companies have around 25,000 billion dollars (25T) in policies (about 80% for life insurance and the rest for non-life insurance) against only $1 - 1.5$T in capital, even before any asset depreciation, which is a really quite a small amount.

In fact, the amount is much too small: a major natural catastrophe, a series of bankruptcies or the nationalization of large banks could trigger the bankruptcy of insurers, which would be even less tolerable than that of the banks: savers (including retirees) would see their holdings vanish; entrepreneurs would no longer find anyone with whom to share risks; companies as well as households would lose a source of financing, at least as equally important as banks.

In other words, the nationalization of banks would precipitate that of the insurance companies. Hiding this reality by changing accounting regulations will do nothing but delay this. Naturally, the G20 has not addressed this in the slightest.

The Recession

As a precaution, households will reduce their consumption even more and keep their savings available. Therefore we will see a drop in real estate and car buying, and a reduction of mortgage loan repayments.

Even though businesses benefit from the significant price drop of raw materials, just like households, they will be confronted by a huge drop in their turnover, a deteriorated social climate, the disinvestments of credit insurers, and a fast-growing working capital and recapitalization.

Banks will not dare to lend with the same audacity as before, including to profitable businesses, because of potential problems they could be hiding, as we have seen. Moreover, the Basel-II Accords will force them to increase their capital provision and the IFRS norms will oblige them to devalue their assets, which would reduce their capacity to lend by the same amount.

In total, the economic slow down, which had started long before the financial crisis with the increase in the price of raw materials, will get worse at least in 2009 and 2010. The sectors the most at risk will be insurance, banking, construction, the automobile industry, airline companies, and luxury department stores. It cannot even be ruled out that some public utilities will go bankrupt. Consequently, unemployment will grow the world over, especially as productivity will continue to increase at a rate over 2% per year. In the United States, unemployment could reach 10% of the working population from June 2009. In France, if no massive measures are taken, unemployment could reach its highest point in history. China could be severely shaken economically and politically if economic growth decreases, which is likely in 2009, to under 6% per year. Finally, those who benefit from oil profits will be seriously affected if the stock market value of crude oil continues to drop.

Everyone will make decisions that will conform only to national interest: nationalizing some companies, subsidizing others, thereby causing the center of interest to shift back to the territory by a different route from that of 1929, but leading to the same disastrous, protectionist effects. At the worst, the WTO accords could even be called into question, which would interrupt all progress in trade liberalization for a long time.

Depression

We cannot exclude the possibility that the recession will become a depression. That is to say that instead of having a world economic growth of 0% in 2009 and 2010, it could plunge down to -5%, -10% or even, in certain sectors, -30%. For some, that seems unthinkable today. However, it has already happened in Japan, at the beginning of the 90s. It is what is already happening in some countries like Germany, Great Britain, Spain and the United States in a certain number of sectors: such as private low-cost housing and the automobile and steel industries. Nothing can keep one from fearing that this may spread in 2009 and 2010 in many other countries.

Besides, such a trend will be encouraged by worldwide reactions created by the consciousness of the magnitude of the threats: all will ask themselves what will happen if the business where they work lost 20% of its turnover, households will prepare for a 20% decrease in income and will set up emergency savings. Directors, at all levels, will cut costs to prepare for it, and some are already cost cutting. For their part, households will consume considerably less. In the same way, banks, which will be expecting such an evolution, will reduce their consumer credits, mortgages and business working capital loans by at least 20%.

This will have two consequences: the less people consume, the less profit businesses will make and the less businesses invest, the less employment they will provide.

In other words, excessive cautiousness will turn a recession into a depression.

Inflation

In the beginning, depression pushes the prices of assets down and creates severe competition between producers and distributors. Businesses will slash the prices of cars, clothes, household objects and housing. There will be sales all year round. In theory, this will have a positive effect on purchasing power.

In the long term, the enormous financial and monetary mass injected into the economy, transferring debt from households to loans granted by penniless states, can only lead to a massive increase in the world monetary mass, that is much higher than the equivalent production.

In the end, despite the efforts of the central banks, we can expect a massive increase in inflation. This will begin suddenly, when we are least expecting it, for example at a time of a sharp increase in the price of oil, pulling currencies into a downward spiral.

This inflation could be hoped for in order to eliminate debts accumulated by households and states, that otherwise could not be balanced. The losers will be those who are not in debt or who are, but at a variable rate.

On a worldwide scale, this inflation would also be a sign of victory of the young, (the majority on the planet), over the old, (the majority in developed countries). It would still be the result of a decision made by the majority, but concerning another electorate, this time all over the world. In this case, the return of inflation would be the first real democratic, global decision.

Since the financial and economic crisis has been caused by excess debt, and since in addition to private debt there is also more and more public debt, the crisis could only be resolved by allowing debtors to spread out their debt, or even to not require them to pay it back at all. For that, many now think that a general increase in prices and wages would be the best solution, because it would reduce the amount allotted for debt in revenue.

This solution may seem impossible: for thirty years, we have been trying to handle inflation everywhere because it drives the poorest, in particular retirees, into ruin and because it denotes a breach in the loyalty between creditors and debtors. Even more than before, with this crisis, we have entered a period of deflation where everyone is holding off spending money, waiting for the prices to drop further – and where the decline in demand, unemployment and the decrease in raw materials are leading to a downward spiral.

This solution could seem plausible: the doubling of the American money supply in twelve months, the enormity of the quantitative easing of central banks can only consequently lead to an increase in demand, which will be confronted with a decrease in offer when the current bankruptcies will have left their mark.

This solution may seem ideal: without anyone having planned or instigated it, debt would lighten, consumers would be incited to spend money at a quicker rate, before prices went up; the economic machine would restart; wages, prices and retirement funds would quickly be indexed; and interest rates would rise.

All those who work, take on debt and have an income would be the winners: employees, buyers of real-estate, companies taking on debt to invest; states, whose value of debt would be reduced; banks themselves would not suffer, because inflation would reduce their liabilities (even if they might suffer some loss connected to their bond portfolios) and because they would earn money by returning to their profession as the intermediary between depositors and borrowers. The same would be true for insurance companies, whose policy commitments to retirees would decrease.

There would also be many victims: creditors, pension funds, holders of non-indexed bonds, retirees whose pensions are not indexable, the wealthy, current account holders and Sovereign Wealth Funds. States would have the most difficulty refinancing themselves with bonds.

The victims, as they have enough political power (wealthy individuals and Sovereign Wealth Bonds), would try to transfer the cost of debt reduction onto the weakest (employees and retirees), and to obtain at least some compensation. For example, we could imagine that, by refusing to lose their assets, Sovereign Wealth Funds would demand a greater political role and would even demand to replace the weakened dollar by a global currency like the SDR, which the Chinese have just requested.

This trend could deteriorate into hyperinflation, if everyone succeeded in protecting themselves with indexation against the inflation of other's income and prices. In this case, we know very well that everyone would lose out, the middle class would be ruined and democracy would not survive.

To avoid this disaster, we need to have the political courage to trigger inflation soon enough for it to be useful, and to start, when its rate goes above 5% per year, a speedy and aggressive price stabilization plan.

This is a dangerous gamble, but it will probably be inevitable in the long run. It is imperative that we consider this now, in order to prevent it from settling in without us having chosen it for ourselves.

Bankruptcy of Developed Countries and the Future of "Chimerica"

An American depression would pave the way for a crash of the world economy of which the United States is still a main player thanks to the money that is lent to it by the rest of the world. Now, no substitute is available like in 1880 when the dollar replaced the pound. No currency would be able to take over, not even the euro, as it has no economic, political and military existence independent of the European Union.

In a certain way, the current financial crisis can also be understood as a major step in the acceleration of the world's loss of confidence in the United States, and in the gradual obligation that has been imposed on the United States and Americans to reimburse their debts, or to declare themselves bankrupt.

That is not a theoretical possibility. Other countries have already found themselves in this situation in the past, like Great Britain at the end of the 19th century or more recently, Argentina. Today, others are waking up in this situation, indebted in intolerable conditions. This is already the case of Iceland, Hungary and the Ukraine. Towns and regions which invested their funds imprudently, or which borrowed within products that have now become "toxic" will be or are already affected.

Tomorrow it will be the case of other Asian or Latin American countries – Mexico, Chile, Korea, Russia,

Malaysia, Kazakhstan – that had or will all have to borrow from the IMF or from sovereign wealth funds, larger and larger sums and at more and more usurious rates. This is already happening particularly to Japan whose public debt exceeds 180% of the GDP and which could suffocate from an unexpected increase in interest rates.

European countries, which have only individual, not collective debt, are not running the same risk, thanks to the euro, whose share in world exchange reserves will increase to the detriment of the dollar. Some of these very indebted countries, like Italy, (which, as we have seen, is now borrowing at a 1% higher interest rate than Germany to raise money), are protected by the existence of the European currency in spite of everything else. However, they would have every cause for concern if countries of the Eurogroup that show a surplus decided to withdraw solidarity towards indebted members, or if they decided to use inflation as a means to finance their economy.

The United States will certainly remain the leading world economy, the most powerful armed forces and the biggest research group for a long time yet. Investors the world over will continue to throw themselves on bonds issued by the American Treasury, which are still graded AAA, for a while yet. However, American public debt (which is over 10T) is being weighed down by the Paulson plan, the Obama plan, and the ongoing financial support of Fannie Mae, Freddie Mac, AIG and others yet to come. The general indebtedness of the country already exceeds the world GDP: 54T. Foreign financiers such as the Chinese, the Arabs, and the Japanese, will hesitate more and more before investing savings in American Treasury bonds. Besides the CDSs linked to these bonds show through the value given to them by the market, that the perception of American default reimbursement probability, albeit weak, has been multiplied by thirty in nine months. The cost of insuring one million dollars worth of American treasury bonds with a CDS has gone from 1,000 to 30,000 dollars. An exchange crisis, which would considerably devalue the dollar, would be one of the realistic consequences of the loss of confidence in American resources.

Exchange Crisis

In 2008 and 2009, What differentiates the 2008 crisis from unlike what has happened formerly during nearly all other financial crises, is that the exchange markets of the principal currencies have evolved in an orderly fashion. The dollar rose compared to the euro, but decreased compared to the Japanese yen, and hardly moved compared to the Chinese yuan, which is not convertible to gold either. The dollar could have been expected to collapse following the explosion of all this debt (particularly external debt), thus forcing the

American Central Bank to increase its interest rates in order to support its stock market value, whilst, it is contrarily forced to decrease its rates in order to support economic growth. Such a decrease in the dollar does not seem to be imminent because China still needs to buy dollars to maintain America's stock market value, therefore preserving its own export capacity.

This might not last. Considering the growth of American debt, and current scarcity of world savings, the dollar will be less and less widely accepted as the reference currency, because savers will be reluctant to invest in the dollar. Today's situation is rather strange, savers are under the obligation to buy dollars, for want of anything better, but they know that the dollar is in jeopardy. Oil producers and other big world trade players will establish their contracts more and more in other currencies, of which the euro. When China really decides to concentrate on its domestic market and redirects its industry in that direction, it will no longer have any reason to defend the parity of the dollar. At which time, the dollar will massively decrease, unless the American Central Bank decides to launch into an interest rate war to avoid an excessive drop. This is unlikely, because of the impact that such an attitude would have on economic growth; the dollar is only holding on because Beijing is letting it. "Chimerica" will only last as long as Beijing needs it to.

All together, the Japanese and the sovereign wealth funds of the Arabs and the Chinese (that have 2.5T of capital today, having lost 0.5T in the crisis and should represent 10T in 2010), would then have the means to buy most of American assets, at a low price and using devalued dollars.

Even though the main risk is for the dollar, a threat for the euro cannot be ruled out. Of course, the euro is protecting members of the Eurogroup from the financial crisis and should, at first, reinforce the integration of these countries and incite new countries to join them. Iceland is now an applicant for entry into the Union and Norway could become one. Denmark, whose currency suffered a lot on October 8, paid a high price for it and is now considering a new referendum on the euro. So are Sweden, Poland, the Czech Republic and Norway itself.

However the refusal of the less indebted countries to support the laxer ones could challenge the very existence of the euro and so could the recent, but very discreet authorization given to a few central banks of the European Union, allowing them to receive stock deposits that they will choose independently – which could practically lead to granting each Eurogroup member country the right to create its own euros!

All this will certainly bring us to rethink money creation in another way, and to wonder about the necessity of a worldwide single currency.

The Social, Ideological and Political Crisis

Ideology, which establishes the power of a group, can only persist if it manages to give a meaning to people's lives, if it gives them a reason to work even if they do not want to. Today liberal ideology would not persuade us that world capitalism benefits more than a small minority. Neither could it make us agree that at the end of 2008, just like all the other years, it was fair to pay 10 billion dollars in bonuses to bankers. Nor will it make us believe that democracy, which is supposed to balance this out, really takes into account the poorest people and the future generations. From now on, democracy and the stock market are going to become values in jeopardy. The ideology of stock market democracy is in peril.

Relatively speaking, the current situation resembles that of the downfall of the Roman Empire, which, as we know, lasted for more than three centuries, leading to a thousand years of chaos. In particular, a change of ideology could lead to the advent of American protectionist, military, almost totalitarian, power, which would probably be mainly theocratic. Theocracy would then be a wincing and caricatural form of future democratic organizations, worrying about the long term, just as fascism and Nazism became demonic caricatures of what would later become social democracy.

In fact, we must not exclude the idea that this crisis could cause protest, through revolt and unprecedented political violence, along with a return of class hatred. After all, does not the crisis strikingly demonstrate the validity of the theories of Marxism; that of flamboyant, global and suicidal capitalism? This crisis will also help us to understand how a small group of people, without producing wealth, managed to appropriate the majority of what was produced, in all legality and without any control. We will also come to understand how this same group, having rounded up everything it could take, managed to make employees, taxpayers, workers, consumers, entrepreneurs, and savers the world over pay for these significant profits, bonuses and subsidies. How the states were forced, within a few weeks to fill the gaps left in this small group's funds, with sums exceeding thousands of times the amounts that the same governments refuse to give to the poorest people in developed countries and the poverty-stricken in the rest of the world.

Certainly, this "confiscation" operates legally, "honestly" and without violence. In the opinion of some, this is what constitutes the main reason for revolt: if all this is legal, the system that allows such aberration should no longer exist!

CHAPTER 5

THE THEORETICAL FRAMEWORK OF CRISES AND SOLUTIONS: THE CONFLICT BETWEEN THE REQUIREMENTS OF DEMOCRACY AND THE MARKETS

The preceding historical overview is comparable to an almost Shakespearian plot, in which the greed of some and the panic of others have collided, dashing the house of cards of our illusions, and only to the benefit of a powerful few.

For my part, I intend to find a deeper explanation, a systemic one. This will show that the answer to the crisis does not lie in pointing fingers at the few who are responsible for it, such as bankers, regulators or governments, it necessitates a veritable revolution of the theoretical framework. As long as analysis and action against the crisis remain based, for the right-wing, only on the regret at having to breach the principles of liberalism, and, for the left-wing, only on seeking the nostalgic return to a welfare state, nothing serious can be undertaken to surmount it.

In fact, we can neither reduce the cause of the crisis to a lack of market regulation nor to the depravity of a few speculators. Neither can it be solely explained by the clash of two social classes. Even if general opposition between employees and owners of capital is stronger than ever, the complexity of the markets, of control means and of payment methods cause social classes to intermingle. Neither can the crisis be only explained by the irrational spiral of fear, the unfair access to information, the laxity of regulators, globalization in itself, the Washington Consensus, or the lack of a state regulator.

The sequence of events leading up to the current crisis began with the widening of social inequalities in the United States and in all developed countries that restricted demand. It has carried on due to American society's implicit decision to use its financial system as a substitute for a fair distribution of income. It has carried on due to the financial system's ability to invent new products without any regulation, leading it to become limitlessly wealthy and limitlessly indebted in order to hide its problems, delay them or export them, in particular via London, an annex of Wall Street and other offshore centers. But this sequence of events alone cannot explain everything; or rather it is explained by a much deeper cause.

Firstly, any crisis is the result of a lack of information. There will always be information asymmetry between the present and the future. It is this asymmetry that causes crises. In addition, unless we wish to have a repetitive world (in itself and its environment), that is to say, a world where information about the future would be, inherently perfect, we can only resign ourselves to handling crises as they come, all the while accepting our fair share of their weight. For that, we must think, forecast and react.

Secondly, this very particular crisis questions, due to its origins, the utility of a banking system. Financial institutions and markets are necessary instruments for the progress of civilizations. They allow the transfer, in principle without theft or despoilment, and against remuneration in interest or dividends, of the savings of those who are able to save to those who could put those savings to better use. To achieve this, banks and markets must be acutely well-informed regarding investment opportunities and able to provide savers with profits in the form of remuneration which could be invested capital or a service, depending on whether the banking system is private or public.

Two opposing deviancies can arise in this system. Firstly, financial institutions give rise to and take part in an artificial fad for very profitable, but very risky investments, by encouraging people to run into debt to acquire them, particularly with a view to boosting pension funds. Conversely, they can keep the information they obtain about the best investments to themselves. In either case, finance is diverted from its function, which is to finance others, and becomes a means of making money, much more than the total profitability of the economy, thanks to information that it can obtain. Hence, the importance of its control by a central bank, which could neither be outsourced, nor downplayed, and must be managed without giving in to the pressure of the substantial political powers behind finance.

Here is where a financial crisis begins: when regulators give free rein to financiers, such as in the afore-mentioned first case (that of an artificial fad), a financial crisis could be triggered when the value of assets reaches an untenable level and if certain players' debt becomes unmanageable through buying these assets. In the second case (the financial system's monopolization of an excessive profit share earned from industrial ventures), an economic and political crisis could be triggered and thus jeopardize society as a whole. In general, these two types of financial crises are triggered one after the other. In either case, finance expounds that it is possible to earn a huge amount of money without producing real goods.

As finance has greatly developed over the centuries, financial crises have increasingly become a warning signal of economic and political crises. Crises are no longer caused solely by shortages, as in the past. Now there are also crises due to over-production, or rather from insufficient demand compared to production capacity, that is to say, proof of the incapacity of a system to guarantee the balanced financing of the economy.

And yet, this does not fully explain everything. It does not explain why certain financial crises are overcome and why others deteriorate into economic crises or why we are today – and only today – in a truly global financial crisis.

In my opinion, to solve these enigmas, we must go back to the driving force of our societies, which is the respect of one value: individual freedom. It is the enhancement of this value which has led to the emergence of our economic and financial systems, and which has brought about their contradictions.

Markets, Democracy and "Insiders"

Century after century, in Northern Europe, then throughout Europe, then around the whole world, we have chosen to favor individual freedom over all other values (justice, solidarity or immortality). For this end, two mechanisms have been set up which, in principle, allow the organization of this freedom within the context of scarcity that defines the human condition: the market and democracy, or rather *the markets* (labor, goods, technologies, capitals) and *democratic levels* (national, regional, municipal...). The market allows the free allocation of rare resources to produce and acquire private goods. Democracy allows the free allocation of rare resources to produce and distribute public goods.

Historically, it has always been a strong non-democratic state that creates markets, which in turn gives rise to a bourgeoisie. The latter, in controlling capital markets (and therefore, in a capitalist society, all other markets as well), thus takes over power through the progressive generalization of democracy.

So markets and democracy strengthen each other. Democracy needs the market because there cannot be political freedom without economic freedom. The market, which is not infallible, fair or even efficient, needs democracy, or at least a state, to protect property rights, intellectual and entrepreneurial freedom, and to make it possible for the means of production to be used to their fullest.

However, whereas democracy is in principle governed by a changing majority which takes hold of and controls the state machine, markets are dominated by those who control the means of production, in particular by those who can allocate capital according to the information at their disposal, the controllers of savings, whom I shall refer to here as the "insiders:" bankers, analysts and private investors.

Here, the word "insiders" does not imply any value judgment. The function they fulfill is useful. They help better allocate savings, which cannot merely be exclusively allocated according to an interest rate, but according to in-depth knowledge of the market outlook. Here, the word "insiders" reflects the fact that information has become one of the most precious resources.

If democracy were perfect, if it could impose equity, each and every person would be equally informed. There would be no need for the "insider," or rather everyone would be one, which amounts to the same thing. It is this lack of equity that has given birth to "insiders," individual non-equitable beneficiaries of a particular commodity: economic and financial information about the profitability of projects.

If everyone were an "insider," society could become organized into a combination of juxtaposed private contracts. Due to the fact that the information about the market is not equal and perfect for every agent, the state must impose a social contract establishing principles of equity and security valid for everyone, to avoid the widening of the inequalities between the "insiders" and the others, and to set up instruments to control their actions. Economic, monetary and budgetary policy could then regulate economic cycles, maintain stable demand, production and employment, and implement regulation, first on currency, then on the markets themselves, to avert the consequences of the cumulative imbalances linked to the monopolization by the "insiders" of the profits linked to their privileged knowledge about risks and potentialities.

The "insiders," who devise new financial instruments, are particularly well positioned to get the best out of them, even when these instruments end up failing. They are neither employees, nor investors. In general, they are transaction arrangers, controllers of savings. These "insiders" can thus appropriate most of the new wealth generated by technological or financial innovations, and sometimes even to the detriment of those who control these companies.

The "insiders" are thus more important, in modern society, than the owners of capital. They hold temporary annuity (information) from which they draw profit and from which they are able to generate growth. Today, they are obviously mostly in the U.S., but, in essence, they are all citizens of the same world: the world of finance. And all the rest ensues.

Disloyalty and the Rule of the Financier

The couple formed by the market and democracy is not, by nature, harmonious. First and foremost, it is founded on individual freedom, trusting the market to be efficient and democracy to handle justice, it downgrades all other values, in particular, solidarity. It praises, in all domains, individual freedom, that is to say, the right to change one's mind. Everything becomes reversible and precarious, even contracts, both for employment and alliances, and therefore so does the social contract. There is no longer any reason to respect a commitment which inhibits our freedom. There is no longer any reason to be loyal to anyone other than ourselves. And in particular, there is no longer any reason to be loyal to future generations... however, our great grandchildren do not have the right to vote! The defense of individual freedom thus makes disloyalty and greed acceptable values; it destroys job stability, also the stability of the law, and thwarts altruism. Those who have information, the "insiders," do not share it, or at least, they use it for their sole benefit before conceding to share it.

Moreover, now everyone, sensing that the system can only survive by defending its own insecurity, is thus caught in a mindset of urgency, of impatience. Foreseeing increasing risk, everyone has tried to get the most and as quickly as possible. This general feeling of insecurity has above all encouraged the "insiders" to stop being loyal to the companies they finance and the households or institutions whose resources they manage; the whole situation has incited them to keep, if they can, any and all occasions they may find to make a profit for themselves.

The Disappearance of the Rule of Law

A major contradiction exists between the two mechanisms that are supposed to serve freedom. First of all, democracy is applicable only to a certain territory, within given borders, whereas, markets are inherently borderless, whether for goods, capital, technologies or labor. Yet, today, global democracy does not exist, nor does a global rule of law in any sector (except for certain sports or certain self-regulating professions such as accountants, or for aviation safety), but on the other hand, there are global markets; which is especially the case with capital markets, more able than any other to evolve quickly and to develop outside a national framework, to slide into the cracks of regulations, to set up here, there and everywhere, notably in the virtual framework of the Internet.

It is also the case of most goods and services markets, and even in labor markets where, despite the reluctance of the masters of other markets, wages are harmonizing and employees are migrating. We could even say that almost all markets are global today, including those which seemed, not that long ago, the most ingrained in national traditions (cuisine, fashion, beauty care, leisure and entertainment etc.).

As markets are global, unlike states which are governed by the rule of law, they are slowly prevailing over the rule of law of each nation and over the democracy which supposedly founded it. The ability to set up the regulation of financial markets disappeared with the competition between financial centers to establish the most beneficial legislation for their "insiders."

We now find ourselves in an unprecedented situation. Whereas in any nation, a strong state creates the market, which, in return, creates democracy, on a global scale the market has created itself without a state having created it or regulated it. We therefore find ourselves, on a global scale, in a situation where no existing institution is able to create a rule of law. There is no Winter Palace to storm! No Bastille Prison to knock down! We are now in a theoretical situation of a perfect and pure market made in such a way that we know it is inherently incapable of being efficient, and only creates sub-optimal situations, which are no longer using productive capacities to their fullest and no longer fairly distributing resources. This is the case today.

As we do not know how to create the rule of law that is needed, lawless zones are multiplying. An "a-legal," illegal and criminal economy, is developing. Everyone is incited to shift what should be in the social contract to the private contract. Public services are and will be increasingly carried out by private entities, including that which concerns security and equity. This leads to a widening gap between access to property, income and information, and the triumph of financial capitalism.

The Triumph of Financial Capitalism

We can now explain how the situation that triggered the current crisis arose through this scenario.

Information becomes less and less equally distributed. Those who have it invent and will continually invent, new financial instruments to access it and to make the most of it. First, this unfair access to information causes excess supply, offset by the debt of non-insiders, which is secured on the value of their property. This leads to an increase in consumption that leads to economic growth and fosters increasing property values, which in turn amplifies debt, beyond that which can be financed by the creation of genuine wealth.

The "insiders" are the main beneficiaries, through the conception of financial instruments that seduce both the poorest borrowers and the richest lenders. The former are unaware that, sooner or later, they will have to pay very high interest rates. The latter are unaware that their savings have been invested in high-risk products. And as for the "insiders", they only have their minds on their annual bonus. The most clear-sighted know that this cannot last, that at a given time, which is still unknown, either the savers will be the victims, or the lenders, and more likely it will be both. Therefore, the "insiders" do everything they can to make investment and borrowing mechanisms as complex as possible and to insure that their own interests are well protected. Moreover, realizing that it cannot last, they allocate themselves an increasing share of national income at the expense of working income, an amount increasing all the faster as the risk is high and the crisis nearing. In other words, according to this theory, the remuneration of the "insiders" increases with the imminence of the crisis and not vice-versa. That is exactly what has happened in today's crisis.

The Triggering of a Financial Crisis

When, for a purely anecdotal purpose, people other than the "insiders" become aware of the intolerable nature of debts and assets, the "insiders" realize that their financial products start losing value. Thus, they try to get out of a system that is upheld only by them, causing a ripple effect followed by a state of panic. Everyone steers clear of debt and scrambles for cash. The financial system freezes. Banks stock money and create a shortage, just as the stockpiling of consumer goods once created shortages in the Soviet system. This stockpiling smothers the economy which then falls into recession and even into depression.

In general, even during such a hard period, the "insiders" manage to keep the situation under their control, to have states fund their losses and save a system from which they have made as much money as they could. They even hope taxpayers will pay the part of their profits that might not yet have been paid by the savers and employers.

The Solution: Rebalancing the Market by a Rule of Law

This analysis perfectly explains the way in which the current financial crisis is unfolding and deteriorating into depression. It was even foreseeable. By applying this approach, the solution to this crisis will entail either going back to markets confined by borders and a national rule of law, that is, to protectionism and competitive devaluations, or instating a rule of law on the level of the global market. This would be a governmental system as democratic as possible, capable of regulating markets, inhibiting a small minority of "insiders" to claim the profits earned from risks and the monopolization of information.

The first solution was attempted in the thirties, and we know how successful that was... Today, it would be even more disastrous due to the greater interweaving of economies, the intensity of the division of labor, and the entanglement of capital, goods and even labor markets.

The second solution requires the markets, at least the financial ones, to be balanced by an efficient rule of law. In particular, it requires supervision mechanisms which insure that the access to information is fairly distributed and available to all. If it is impossible to completely withdraw the privileged access to information held by some, it will at least be necessary to moderate it. To accomplish this, we will have to instate an obligation on a global scale, forcing those who make others run a risk to also accept their fair share of the risk, as well as implement a supervision of liquidity requirements. We will have to restrict forward markets to only conducting genuine economic activities, and probably cancel some of the "insiders'" debts. Together, we will have to draft the definition of a "bad bank" (its perimeter, its methods of determining the value of assets).

We must decide on a foreseeable, contractual and loyal partition of the world's savings, imposing reduction of the debt of the countries without reserves up to a level that can be financed by their actual real production. We will also have to restrict the profits demanded by "insiders," so that they do not exceed the real profitability of the economy. We may even have to go as far as a socialization of supervisory functions, such as the rating system. This would not be a measure of reprisal – but the only way to make the market work while maintaining control over it.

This is under the assumption that a truly global policing and justice system is also set up, capable of controlling and sanctioning any breach of its rules.

Finally, it will be necessary to implement on a global scale what has worked on a national scale in some countries: large-scale public projects and a support system for the creation of small-scale companies. In particular, to develop communication networks to inform the greatest number of economic players regarding what is afoot and to make it possible for everyone to become an "insider."

Is this a utopian ideal? Of course it is! However, the fact remains that this is the one and only solution, and it must be implemented with the utmost urgency! Unless we resign ourselves, once again, to waiting for the crisis to worsen, to the degree that people will completely lose their confidence in the markets, for democracy itself to be declared incapable of controlling the "golem" it has created. It is the ideal of individual freedom, which has founded both of them, that would thus be called into question once again.

Thus this utopia is of real and extreme urgency. After all, why can't we manage to quickly set up a system of governance for finance as efficient as that which has been set up for aviation safety or soccer?

CHAPTER 6

AN EMERGENCY PLAN

The financial crisis is still controllable. This generation has the human, financial and technological means at its disposal to ensure that this is merely a slight setback.

The severity of the threats looming over the global economy and the theoretical analysis presented above plead the case for the implementation of a coherent action plan in every country, particularly in those where the derivatives of the capital markets have wreaked havoc. This action plan could be defined by one single ambition: to rebalance the power of markets by the power of democracy on a national, continental and global scale. The first step is to rebalance the power of the financial markets by a rule of law.

Some have spoken of the need for a new Bretton Woods. However, currencies are not the most urgent point to address, even if the stabilization of the dollar will become necessary and even if the creation of a single global currency may have its day – and this sooner than we think. Many other much more pressing subjects require a series of reforms if we want to stave off depression.

Logically, we should begin by instating stricter governance of the global financial system to bring back transparency and confidence. Some will claim there are inherent dangers in having another layer of bureaucracy. This is a wrongful perception. Any human organization – whether it is a company, or better yet, a bank – is a "bureaucracy." The question is rather to know on behalf of whom it is acting and to know if it is sufficiently controlled to fulfill its functions in the most efficient way. As far as finance is concerned, what has been mentioned above shows that constant regulation better adapted to the ingenuity of markets and the evolution of technologies must set limits to risk, which is required for growth, without eliminating it in the process.

More than ever, the world needs billions of creators, innovators and entrepreneurs who can take risks in complete freedom, though within the limits of not infringing on the freedom of others. However, obviously nobody could think that financial capitalism will adopt a code of ethics all by itself. At the moment, it is ready to do anything, or almost anything, to make taxpayers fear enough for their own future to accept, without too much reticence, to finance its errors. But, as soon as it can, it will recover its splendor and start to develop its own interests again, by inciting others to pile up debt for its exclusive benefit. Therefore, the problem is not to impose a code of ethics on capitalism, but to integrate it into a system governed by a rule of law.

What has been laid out above shows that the supervision of finance is a task in everyone's interest and must not be left, even partly, in the hands of the private sector, nor even in the hands of one government which could impose rules conforming to its own interests, but which could be disastrous to others. Detailed and constantly reassessed global regulation would give us the possibility to anticipate imbalance and in particular to inhibit public funds from being used to recapitalize banks. It's time we understood that this crisis could be the chance for us to save the world, a last warning sign before a catastrophe that an anarchic globalization could trigger. It's time we asked a few simple questions such as: can we set up on a global scale what has worked for a while on a national scale? Could we create a global state (that is, a supranational administration and a policing and justice system) from scratch? Should we create a Keynesian state on a global level? Should we revive worldwide growth, wasteful in resources, or should we opt for weak growth, for the sake of the environment?

In accordance with the preceding analysis, it will be necessary to first restore order in each national economy; first and foremost in the one where everything started off: the American economy. Then we will need to set up supranational regulation and governance. Finally, we will need to launch great worldwide projects aimed at re-orientating growth. To accomplish this, we must all agree to carry out the complete set of measures hereinafter outlined, in ascending order of their difficulty to implement, and which unfortunately also inversely corresponds to the ascending order of the urgency. Listing them suffices to show how much the current debates are far off the mark:

Restore Order in Each National Economy

In every country, the crisis requires that order be reinstated in public finances.

This must begin with the country where everything comes from and goes back to, the United States. President Barack Obama has come to power at a time when everyone, in America, is becoming aware of the gravity of the crisis looming. Just like Franklin Roosevelt when he arrived at the White House at the beginning of the Great Depression, or like Ronald Reagan when he took over power at the start of the Fordism crisis, Barack Obama must launch a global action plan to restart the economy, and all other countries must, for their part, adapt it to their specific situation. This action plan, which must go much further in the United States than what was decidedplanned by the G20 and Geithner plan, would aim to:

• rebuild the capital of banks, strongly encourage interbank lending, maintain liquidity and restore the creditworthiness of banks and give, if necessary, a blanket guarantee on all deposits; oblige banks to abide by counter-cyclical capital requirements, unlike what the Basel-II Accord dictates, and allow less volatile accounting of financial institutions which are funded in the long term, by more strictly defining Tier 1 shareholder equity, leaving only real capital;

• prohibit financial instruments based on the value of speculative assets; require banks to keep a share of the risk linked to the riskiest financial products in their balance sheets, particularly debts they securitize; prohibit private equity players from borrowing more than a few times what they invest, and prohibit certain short-selling mechanisms, in particular for banks;

• dare to nationalize, at least partially, certain banks by taking control and confining "toxic" products in ad hoc structures; fight against the reconstitution of banking oligopolies, and prohibit excessive remuneration of financial system players, all the while requiring bonuses to be calculated over several years;

• support private demand in the long term by increasing minimum wages, strengthening union powers and reforming income taxation;

• support troubled industrial sectors, at least to the same degree as we have supported banks, under the condition they modernize and adapt to environmental requirements;

• provide capital to SMEs so they can modernize;

• set up a social security system in the United States which can insure sick leave income continuance and cover healthcare expenses; extend the length of unemployment benefits;

• stabilize the housing market at a lower, yet stable, price; set up a moratorium on loans, in particular mortgage loans, involving the refinancing of all mortgage loans by a state body similar to the Home Owners' Loan Corporation, a key element of Roosevelt's New Deal in 1933;

• restore credibility and respectability to the engineering and research sectors and conversely revert the profession of banking back to being modest and boring, something it should never have stopped being; with that aim in mind, also strictly supervise finance sector salaries;

• have the evolution of the value of movable and immovable assets included in the definition of inflation, which can no longer be defined only by the evolution of consumer products;

• significantly increase savings rates through taxation to facilitate debt repayment;

- massively and progressively reduce the debt of all players for it to go down from 4350 % to at least 100 % of the GDP;
- carry out this plan by guaranteeing ad hoc tax revenue so that the budget deficit in the United States does not exceed 1T, as it is most likely at today.

Thiese types set of measures should firstly be applied in the United States, then in each country concerned, notably in Japan and Europe.

As for France, such a plan falls into the framework of the propositions of the Committee for the Liberation of French Growth, whose full application is urgently needed more than ever.

Strengthen European Regulation

In each member state, Europe will need to apply the reforms presented above and equip itself with specific regulation instruments. Indeed, how could Europe legitimately demand the reform of the international monetary system if it is not also capable of setting up institutions adapted to its own level?

Certainly, Europeans already have a single currency, which has proven to be a formidable tool these last few months; and a common competition policy which should also be applied to banking, yet no aspect of these brings them closer to European financial governance. Europeans have not even begun in the slightest way to harmonize national policies in all of these sectors. Many derivative products are prohibited in some countries, but authorized in others. Many speculative practices are encouraged in some financial centers, but lambasted in others. Europe does not even have a common definition of the concept of a tax haven or an offshore financial center. Nor does it have a common conception of capital taxation, common regulation of forward exchange markets or hedge funds or a common authority for regulating financial markets. There is no European equivalent of the AMF or the SEC, and the directives in this regard have yet to be finalized. In many regulatory domains, Europeans submit to what comes from Wall Street, the Fed, the SEC, the American Department of the Treasury, and (especially in terms of accounting) ad hoc institutions, greatly controlled by American actors or submitted to rules or the absence of rules of the City which, in this domain, constitutes the most exotic offshore center!

European Union member states, or at least those in the Eurogroup, should thus equip themselves with community institutions (and not only a network of national regulatory authorities) capable of supervising all European players (even and especially those that are not banks), forbidding their financial institutions to work with financial offshore centers and tax havens located outside the Union, and prohibiting, according to common definitions, certain practices from being carried out within the Union, particularly in the City.

In addition to this, they will need to equip themselves with a last resort European lender which should not be the European Central Bank, national governments or the European Investment Bank, but a new entity whose mission would be to guarantee troubled European financial institutions, if they are viable, and have the possibility of participating in their capital and providing subordinated debt.

To prevent them from undermining the entire process of European construction by allowing financial institutions to only work in the national interests of their own public shareholders, the European Commission should effectively have a nationalization tool at its level, that we could call "unionization," and it should also be able to isolate the "toxic" assets of European banks which could reduce the value of the shareholder equity of these banks' capital in an ad hoc structure, as was very successfully done in Sweden in 1992.

Today, nothing legally allows the Commission to become a shareholder of companies, or even to oppose changes to Tier 1 standards by central banks. Nor does anything grant it the possibility of financing such an expense from its bleeding budget, capped at an increase of 1.28 % of European GDP. If we want to prevent the anxiety over the solidity of the European banking system from being added to the concern that is to be expected over the solvability of certain governments, it will nonetheless probably be necessary to come to that.

If the Union does not do this (and there are little chances it will, given its current mood), there are little chances the G20 or the G24 will in turn. All this will end by merely patching things up before the arrival of a much graver new crisis.

Set Uup a Global Financial Regulation System

It is not yet imaginable to use the IMF to set up a single world currency. Nor is it completely necessary to envisage replacing or complementing it with other authorities to control the global financial system. On the contrary, we must bring together all supervisory powers, which are scattered today, and considerably strengthen them. Consequently, the IMF must:

• become the place where all national authorities agree on financial reforms to be carried out in their own countries, including the following;

• have the means to really be the last resort lender (today, there is only .25 T to assist the whole world, which is an absurd amount!). For this we will probably have to raise a specific tax on financial institutions and their dealings, inspired by the Tobin tax;

• become the place where a veritable supranational financial regulation can be set up; for this the IMF will have to establish a *global financial regulation system* compelling every county, including tax havens to abide by the rules outlined above, and a global procedure on the exchange of taxation and financial information;

• take on the role held by the incestuous informality of the Bank for International Settlements which should have disappeared in 1945 because of the role it played with the Nazis, and which has remained a secret, closed-off club of a few central bankers;

• decide to harmonize the amount of guaranteed deposits and shareholder equitycapital, the perimeter and the valuation of potential "bad banks", a global regulation of "derivatives", in particular CDSs; the replacement of the Basel-II Accords on the requirements of bank capital and International Financial Reporting Standards (IFRS) by fairly negotiated international standards;

• supervise rating agencies which should become not-for-profit organizations;

• make it a condition that, in order to be able to operate as a financial institution, anywhere in the world, an authorization must be granted by a country which, being an IMF member, adheres to the global financial regulation system;

• have concrete and efficient procedures for international judicial assistance to enforce this financial regulation, and to establish a common definition of offshore financial centers. In particular, the IMF will have to fight against the reconstitution of banking oligopolies in each country, and systemize the traceability of financial products;

• have the necessary authority to restructure the sovereign debt of every country, including the U.S., and thus assist the reorientation of their economic policies. The IMF will also have to play a role in the policies of harmonizing interest rates and, for that, to require central banks to fight against assets inflation, which must not increase faster on average than wages;

• supervise the transfer of the wealth of savers towards investment centers so that it is used for the genuine production of wealth, and ensure that it is not misappropriated by the financial system. In particular, the IMF will have to study the sources of long-term saving, including those of oil producing countries, which are mostly able to invest outside their borders rather than within.

Finally, the IMF must start considering a single global currency, following the model of Keynes' *bancor*, or a group of currencies including at least the dollar, the yen, the renminbi and the euro. One day, this single currency should take over from the dollar, whose fall seems inevitable. Without this, protectionism will inevitably return.

International Governance

In all logic, to establish balance between the market and democracy, which is a condition for harmonious global development, we must create the instruments required to exercise global sovereignty: a parliament (one man, one vote), a government, worldwide enforcement of the Universal Declaration of Human Rights and its subsequent protocols, the implementation of the decisions of the International Labor Organization in terms of labor law, a central bank, a single currency, global taxation, global law enforcement and justice, a global minimum wage, global raters, and global regulation of the financial markets.

*

*   *

Obviously, all of this is still out of reach, and will be for quite some time. Indeed, as was the creation of the United Nations on the eve of World War II. And we may have to wait for a much more appalling war for the perspective of such reforms to be taken seriously.

Large-scale Worldwide Public Works

The international economy, supervised by such a regulatory system, could suffer from the same crises as those which ultraliberalism gives rise to in every country. To prevent such a result from happening, we will need to place this plan within the framework of a concrete project for society, for the benefit of real people. It will be necessary to give a global state the means, much greater than those currently held by the World Bank, to coordinate social justice and to initiate large-scale public works at an international level, allowing counter-cyclical investment which would duly compensate for the excess of optimism and the excess of pessimism.

In particular, these large-scale public works should be aimed at assisting a massive reorientation of the economy towards non-polluting activities, towards renewable energies, telecommunications and urban infrastructure. They should also contribute to developing equitable information networks. These large-scale projects could be funded by a tax on greenhouse gas emissions.

*
*   *

It is likely that we will follow through with none or almost none of the above. Unless a catastrophe (which nobody would ever wish for) imposes an agonizing reappraisal, nobody, and especially the U.S., will agree to a supranational solution. It took a thousand years of internal warring for Europeans somewhat to resign themselves to the idea. We have not yet had a thousand years of world wars...

At first, we thus have to content ourselves with the hope of setting up modest international governance. This could work if the following five decisions are made in haste:

1. Enlarge the G8 to G24;

2. Merge the G24 and the Security Council into a "Governance Council" bringing together economic power and political legitimacy;

3. Put the International Monetary Fund, the World Bank and other international financial institutions under the authority of this Governance Council;

4. Reform the composition of the boards and the voting rights of international financial institutions, including the IMF and the World Bank, to reflect the new Security Council;

5. Equip these institutions with adequate financial resources.

.

CHAPTER 7

THE FINAL WARNING, PROMISES FOR THE FUTURE

If the colossal task drawn out in the previous chapter is not implemented, if we are content with a timid fix-up job in the hopes of overriding a long recession, in spite of everything we cannot rule out the possibility of the crisis blowing over two or three years from now, of the U.S. continuing to attract all the world's capital and regaining the upper hand, once again leaving financial markets act as they please. Technical progress will prove to be a formidable growth driver. Thus, with cowardly relief, we will forget about all of these stakes. That is, until new bubbles develop to create new income, leading to the outburst of new financial and economic crises, and along with them, outbreaks of violence.

Maybe then we will finally grasp how to seize the amazing opportunities found in new technologies to invent a new world.

Financial Crises to Come

Beyond the current crisis, inequalities will widen, new financial tools will attract savings, and debt with start growing again. New international financial crises may arise. These crises will latch onto a new sort of finance, radically different from that of today, much more integrated and versatile in nature, using all the resources of new communication technologies.

Even if the smaller specialized firms, such as those offering financial advisory services and often associated with an individual or a family, carry on orchestrating mergers and acquisitions, even if the top financial institutions carry on inventing products rendered possible by future technologies, in particular by Internet commerce, it will soon be possible to conduct banking transactions in a completely different way. Especially with the mobile telephone: it already allows 4 billion people to communicate, and far more than 10 million (in particular clients of microfinance institutions) to conduct simple banking transactions.

Its potential market is enormous. Today, 88 % of the world's inhabitants do not have access to a means of investing their savings, 63 % do not have access to credit, and almost as many do not have access to insurance.

Money transfers by mobile telephone will amount to at least 140 billion dollars in five years' time. In the near future, the mobile telephone will even allow more than

6 billion individuals to pay for purchases, manage their bank and savings accounts, even their term deposit accounts, invest on the stock market and create ultra-sophisticated products all by themselves. One day, anyone, even the least knowledgeable, will be able to calculate derivatives and devise structured products over their telephone. Even the very concept of the "insider" will therefore evolve.

It is this change that will completely revolutionize financial markets all over the world. First, telecommunications companies, the owners of computer files and technologies, will be in a position to compete with banks, that is, if they choose not to join forces with them. Then such new financial products, at first generated by microcredit, will pop up everywhere, fully adapted to these future mobile telephones. This will allow billions of people to participate in financial markets directly or through intermediaries – the "insiders." This will massively accelerate the assimilation of the world's poorest into the global market.

Finally, the current supervisory bodies, or those which will be created according to the principles detailed above, will have much difficulty to understand the evolutions of these markets, to control the legal nature of these transactions and even the amount of currency issued by these exchanges, and also to ward off imbalances. Some regulators (for example India, China and Mexico) already require these transactions to go through bank accounts. Monetary control and banking supervision will entail infringing on privacy rights in order to find out exactly what people are doing with their telephones.

This is what will create new types of "insiders" and new forms of the market that are still hard to conceive of today, and in turn forms of financial crises even more harder to ward off. In any case, in less than twenty years' time, worldwide financial crises will be entirely generated by this complex global system encompassing finance and communication technologies.

Other Dangers: the Future of Complex Global Systems

The market, a complex system composed of the planet's billions of inhabitants, is not the only complex global system. The current crisis should at least be the occasion to become aware that the interdependence of the world's billions of inhabitants and the billions and billions of machines amassed in complex systems has already become practically irreversible.

Even at present, we can easily deduce that other terrible events could threaten us if other complex non-financial systems managed to get out of control and remain unforeseeable, such as the case of today's financial system.

This could be the epidemiological system, deteriorating into an uncontrollable pandemic. This could also particularly be Above all, this could turn out to be the most important of imaginable complex systems: the climate. A massive deregulation of the climate could unleash an equally uncontrollable situation and a state of panic similar to what we are currently witnessing on the financial markets.

The issue would obviously be much graver than the one we are talking about here. At the very worst, the deregulation of the financial system could provoke a large-scale depression, hundreds of millions of unemployed workers and a major war; whereas a potential climate disaster could wipe out humanity.

First, here are some facts and figures: the cost of the environmental impact of greenhouse gas emissions (these "toxic" products, employing the word also used to define financial derivative products) was estimated at 3T, which is the same degree as the current losses from the financial crisis. A report made by the European Commission details that every year the global economy wastes 5T only on account of deforestation. However, nobody is taking the problem seriously. And yet, while we managed to find 4T in one month to save the world's banking system, we have never been able to free up the mere 0.02T per year that it would take to fight world hunger effectively, or to save the Brazilian rainforest, or to offer micro-credit to 600 million families that would put this money to better use!

These sums are still accessible today, and so these issues are still manageable. However, in the near future, due to collective indifference and the "positive attitude" of those in power, the impact of the deregulation of the climate can only worsen, and, temperature levels, ocean levels, the melting of glaciers, and the strength of storms along with it.

If climatic deregulation accelerates as fast as the financial crisis has snowballed, we will realize that, just as with the global economy, not only is there no pilot on the plane, there is not even a cockpit. The rise and fall in temperature would become definitive and no human action, no amount of money, however great it might be, could prevent the poles from melting, deserts from expanding, sea levels from rising, and hurricanes from gaining in number and strength. Animal species would go extinct, under-water life would practically cease to exist and unknown types of insects would appear. Hundreds of millions of people would be forced to move, heading aimlessly inland from the coasts. Temperature rates could even increase by more than the 4, 6 or 8 degrees mentioned in the most pessimistic hypotheses, resulting in a large part of the planet becoming uninhabitable; natural phenomena could even cause methane deposits under the ocean floor to break open, releasing massive emissions into the air, quickly asphyxiating all of mankind leaving us with no time to react or find some kind of refuge, including for the richest elites or the best informed.

It would then be too late to moan about not having listened to those who had sounded the alarm (starting with the authors of the Meadows report in 1972); to regret not having reacted when there was still time; to kick ourselves for not having taken the modest, limited and perfectly bearable measures, which would have been enough to reverse the trends and relaunch stimulate a formidable wave of growth based on simple technologies, which are available today, allowing to massively reduce greenhouse gas emissions.

This hypothesis is extreme. But, not any more than the hypothesis of the subprime crisis, announced by several experts, leading to a general loss of control over derivative products, "toxic" or not, and the almost complete freeze on interbank credits, the bankruptcy of banks, companies and nations, as well as a massive, lengthy and uncontrollable global depression, which is now threatening us.

In both cases, we find ourselves confronted with a complex global system, a sort of "golem," without an intention or goal, capable of both serving mankind for the better and of destroying everything in its path, because no ethical consideration is driving it.

As with facing any "golem," it's time we used our common sense of good and evil to control it before it eludes us. It's time we turned this threat into an opportunity.

To this end, we should take advantage of this crisis to become aware of four simple, but often forgotten, truths:

• Everyone, as he is free to do, goes as far as possible to serve his own interests, even to the detriment of his own descendants;

• Mankind can only survive if every person realizes that he or she has an interest in the greater welfare of others;

• Work, in any form, especially with altruistic aims, is the only justification for the appropriation of wealth;

• Time is the only truly rare commodity; any activity that contributes to increasing its availability and using it to its fullest should be particularly well-paid.

If this crisis can help us better absorb these obvious facts that reach well beyond the world of finance, the potential harm will once again become a source of good and this deviation will be at the origin of its control. We may even be able to hope for an affluent world where the markets will only be efficient building blocks, and no longer the absolute masters that they are today.

A world where the only crises will be those in our private lives with sorrow and happiness, its reassuring routine and its glorious surprises.

GLOSSARY

ABS (asset-backed securities): securities backed by assets, created through securitization. ABSs are sometimes made of a portfolio of mortgage loans.

Rating Agency: a firm that assesses the financial soundness of states, companies and financial instruments, by assigning them a grade. The three largest international rating agencies are Moody's, Standard & Poor's and Fitch Ratings.

Alt-A: mortgages granted to lenders who have not had serious repayment problems in the last 24 months (contrary to subprimes).

Arbitrage: is the practice of earning profit from a price differential that could temporarily occur between two similar assets (for example a share or a derivative of one).

BCE: European Central Bank.

Certificates of deposit: short-term securities equivalent to commercial money of companies.

CDO (collateralized debt obligation): securities founded on the securities of several assets, generally ABSs (asset-backed securities) (notably RMBS), shares and bonds.

CDS (credit default swap): an insurance contract between two entities against a risk incurred by one of the two entities, for example an unpaid debt. The price of the CDS demonstrates the confidence granted in the issuer of a loan and serves as a basis to set the value.

Covered bonds: are bonds backed by mortgages or public sector loans. If the issuer defaults on a payment, the investor can be reimbursed by the guaranteed assets.

Derivative: a derivative (a derivative product or contract) is a contrat by mutual agreement, which defines the future financial flow between the buyer and the seller, and whose value is based on an underlying asset. There are different types of derivatives such as futures, swaps, and options.

Senior subordinated notes: a bond whose repayment depends on that of high level and quality investors (seniors).

FED (Federal Reserve Bank): American Central Bank.

Hedge funds: an investment fund characterized by risky investment strategies and derivative products. Hedge funds are often based in tax or regulatory havens.

LBO (leveraged buy out): a purchasing transaction through leverage. A group of investors (often private equity funds) takes over a company, mainly via a loan paid back with the future profits of the company.

Monoline: a financial institution that guarantees a loan by bestowing the lender's own rating grade on the borrower.

Rating: a grade attributed to a state, a company or a security by a rating agency in relation to its financial soundness and meant to indicate to the market the interest rate spread that should be applied.

Private equity: is an activity consisting, for investment funds, of acquiring a share of the capital (equity, as opposed to debt) in operating companies that are not usually listed on the stock exchange.

Repo (repurchase agreement): a transaction of asset buying consisting of selling bonds, shares or another security to another party, in general to a central bank, at a specified fixed rate for a specified fixed time. At term, the seller must buy back the assets by paying back the loan.

RMBS (residential mortgage-backed securities): a type of bond backed by a group of mortgage loans including subprimes, Alt-As or primes. The holder of an RMBS receives the repayments of capital and interest on mortgages that are securitized.

SEC (US Securities and Exchange Commission): the official American agency responsible for financial market regulation.

Spread: the difference between two values that usually measures the risk factor.

Subprime: a mortgage loan for borrowers who have had many repayment problems in the twenty-four months preceding the granting of a loan, lacking a stable job or already heavily in debt (credit card debts, student loans, car loans...).

OTHER WORKS BY JACQUES ATTALI

After t he Crisis What is the future Fayard, 2009

From Cristal to smoke Fayard for French version, 2008

Ghandi a Biography 2007, Fayard, 2007

A Brief History of the Future, Fayard, 2006.

Karl Marx, biography, Fayard, 2005.

The Human Pathway, Fayard, 2004.

The Nomadic Man, Fayard, 2003.

Blaise Pascal: the French Genius, Fayard, 2000.

Noise, PUF, 1977, new edition Fayard, 2000.

Fraternity, Fayard, 1999.

Les Portes du Ciel, play, Fayard, 1999.

La Femme du menteur, novel, Fayard, 1999.

Atlantic Books, 1999.

Dictionary of the 21st Century, Fayard, 1998.

Labyrinth in Culture and Society: Pathways to Wisdom, English Translation, North

Beyond Nowhere, novel, Fayard, 1997.

Mémoires de sabliers, éditions de l'Amateur, 1997.

Verbatim II, Fayard, 1995.

Verbatim III, Fayard, 1995.

Manuel, l'enfant-rêve (illustrations by Philippe Druillet), Stock, 1995.

Europe(s), Fayard, 1994.

He Will Come, novel, Fayard, 1994.

The Economy of the Aapocalypse, Fayard, 1994.

Verbatim I, Fayard, 1993.

1492, Fayard, 1991.

Horizon Lines, Fayard, 1990.

The First Day After Me, novel, Fayard, 1990.

Eternal Life, *novel*, Fayard, 1989.

Literally and Metaphorically, Fayard,1988.

Sigmund Warburg: A Man of Influence, Fayard, 1985.

Fraser's Figure, Fayard, 1984.

A History of Time, Fayard, 1982.

The Three Worlds, Fayard, 1981.

Cannibalism and Civilization, Grasset, 1979.

The New French Economy, Flammarion, 1978.

The Word and the Tool, PUF, 1976.

An Anti-Economic Approach (with Marc Guillaume), PUF, 1975.

Political Models, PUF, 1974.

An Economic Analysis of Political Life, PUF, 1973.